On Jordan's Stormy Banks

Other Titles in the *Real Voices, Real History*™ *Series*

JOHN F. BLAIR, PUBLISHER
Winston-Salem, North Carolina

On Jordan's <u>Stormy Banks</u>

Personal Accounts of Slavery in Georgia

EDITED BY ANDREW WATERS

Published by John F. Blair, Publisher

*The paper in this book meets the guidelines
for permanence and durability of the
Committee on Production Guidelines for
Book Longevity of the Council on
Library Resources.*

Library of Congress Cataloging-in-Publication Data
On Jordan's stormy banks : personal accounts of slavery in Georgia /
edited by Andrew Waters.

p.   cm.   —   (Real voices, real history series)
ISBN 0-89587-228-5 (alk. paper)

1. Slaves—Georgia—Biography. 2. Slaves—Georgia—Social conditions—
19th century. 3. Afro-Americans—Georgia—Interviews. 4. Afro-Americans—Georgia—Social conditions—19th century. 5. Georgia—Biography.
I. Waters, Andrew, 1970– II. Series.
E445.G3 O5 2000
976.8'04'08625—dc21
00-062104

*Cover photograph from the Library of Congress,
U.S. Farm Security Administration Collection (LC-USF 34-17943-C)
Design by Debra Long Hampton*

For Anne

Contents

Introduction

A person's voice has always held more power over us than words alone.

The Reverend Martin Luther King left a legacy of words and deeds that will surely endure as long as there is an American consciousness. Yet when the man's name is mentioned—or perhaps more accurately, when one is asked to quantify his message—what one hears is his eloquent vision echoing down over the congregation gathered on Washington's Great Lawn, the deep, resonant bass of his assured voice: "I have a dream. . . ."

Similarly, President John F. Kennedy embodied the spirit of youthful optimism that the best parts of his administration came to represent when he, in his distinctive Massachusetts accent, exhorted Americans to "ask not what your country can do for you; ask what you can do for your country."

Of course, the voice that can capture the spirit and imagination of an entire country is a special, rare thing. On a much smaller scale, it is not an exaggeration to say that the words we remember most are attached to the gentle, loving tones of a parent, the wise, considered cadence of a favorite teacher, or the excited patter of a soul mate.

That same power, I believe, is the strength of these slave narratives. In simple, often unconsidered words, these accounts capture the essence of a culture in not one but two of our nation's darkest chapters—the period before, during, and after the Civil War and the Great Depression. They describe lives of hard work and abuse, fear and oppression, bringing a unique immediacy to the horrors of slavery and the difficult conditions endured by former slaves after the war. What's more remarkable, however, is that these narratives also describe lives of optimism and perseverance and joy. This is in no way a claim that the conditions of slavery weren't inhumane at best, horrific at worst. It is a claim that these narratives give voice to an aspect of slavery that is often excised from the pages of history: the slaves' humanity.

Often, these two ends of the human perspective—terror and joy—occur within the same narrative, uttered within the same conversation. When eighty-four-year-old Mollie Kinsey describes the fate of her sister, it is impossible not to feel the cold chill of horror: "My sister was given away when she was a girl. She told me and Ma that they'd make her go out and lay on a table, and two or three white men would have innercourse with her before they'd let her get up. She was just a small girl. She died when she was still in her young days, still a girl." In just a few moments, however, the mood changes when Kinsey gives this account: "When I married my second husband, I sho' married a wealthy man. I 'member I went into the smokehouse, and when I saw all that meat, hams, shoulders, lard, and sausage in that house, I said, 'Lawdy, is all this mine?'" While most of us can hardly comprehend the evil described in Kinsey's account of her sister's death, few have not experienced the unadulterated joy of discovering unexpected riches, recognizable in Kinsey's reaction to her newfound treasure.

Similar moments are to be found throughout these narratives. In some cases, the hardships of slavery are perfectly embodied in brief, unadorned accounts like Sally Brown's description of childbirth: "We didn't go to no hospitals like they does now. We just had our babies and had a granny to catch 'em." In other passages, the whole of life's experience—highs and lows—is seemingly captured within just a few sentences, as in the conclusion to Abner Griffin's narrative: "I've never suffered for nothing in my life. I tells you, though, God sho' got me in His hands now. I was thirty-one years when I left the Griffin place to make my fortune. Now I ain't got nothing, ain't doin' nothing, don't know where I going to get nothing. Looks like I made a disfortune instead of fortune!"

For preserving these remarkable voices, we have the

Federal Writers' Project to thank. Created in the midst of the Great Depression as part of the U.S. Works Progress (later Work Projects) Administration (WPA), the agency provided work to jobless writers and researchers throughout the country. Recognizing the importance of capturing the memories of former slaves, most of whom were in their eighties and nineties, the project established a network of field workers assigned to the task of identifying and interviewing these elderly men and women. In the age before tape recorders, workers were sent into the field with only a list of questions, pencil, and paper. The interviews were transcribed in longhand, then typed.

The slave narratives were one of the Federal Writers' Project's many great successes. More than two thousand narratives were eventually collected from seventeen states. These interviews were gathered at the Library of Congress under the title *Slave Narratives: A Folk History of Slavery in the U.S. from Interviews with Former Slaves.* The quality of the individual narratives varies. Many interviewers took great pains to capture the dialects of the slaves, with varying degrees of effectiveness. Others avoided the issue of dialect altogether by writing third-person accounts. Some interviewers used a mix of first-person quotes and third-person exposition. Some of the narratives are quite long and cover a wide range of time periods and experiences, while others can hardly be considered interviews at all.

Although the Federal Writers' Project was farsighted in its collection of this valuable material, it wasn't as prescient in its plans to distribute it. For years, the documents were available only in the Rare Book Room of the Library of Congress, or on microfilm for a fee of $110. In 1972, scholar George P. Rawick published a complete edition of the narratives, grouped according to the states. He titled it *The American Slave: A Composite Autobiography*. Rawick later discovered a large quantity of material that was never submitted to the Library of Congress and was being warehoused in various state and local institutions. He collected these additional narratives and published them in 1979 as a ten-volume supplement to his original series.

My own introduction to the slave narratives was the three-volume set compiled by Belinda Hurmence, a writer, researcher, and schoolteacher in North Carolina. Hurmence read the narratives as research for a historical novel and realized the need to make the material available to the general public in a form that was less intimidating than microfilm or large, multivolume works. In 1984, she published a collection of twenty-one North Carolina slave narratives titled *My Folks Don't Want Me to Talk about Slavery*. That collection was followed by a similar South Carolina collection, *Before Freedom, When I Just Can Remember*, and a Virginia collection, *We Lived in a Little Cabin in the Yard*. I am indebted to Hurmence for striking upon a formula that makes these narratives so accessible to readers.

The purpose of this book is to provide a human perspective on slavery, not a historical one, but before undertaking these narratives readers may find it helpful to understand the environment in which the majority of Georgia's slaves lived. The history of slavery in Georgia is tied to the history of cotton, the state's most important crop in the antebellum period. Rice was the staple crop on the coastal plantations in the colonial period, but as trade with England evaporated in the wake of the American war for independence, sea-coast planters increasingly turned to cotton, which was widely demanded throughout the young United States. White settlers on the western frontier found that cotton thrived in Georgia's upland area as well. As cotton farms became larger and larger, the state's demand for slaves increased. The plantation system quickly found a home in Georgia. In 1800, there were 59,406 slaves in the entire state. By 1860, that number had grown to 462,198.

An excellent example of the conquest of the region by the plantation system is Houston County, located in the state's south-central cotton belt. In 1825, just 4 of the county's slaveholders reported having between 50 and 99 slaves. By 1859, that number had grown to 45 slaveholders. During that period, the county's total slave population grew from 3,741 to 11,797. Readers may find it helpful to bear these figures in mind, for they illustrate that many of the men and women introduced in this book grew up among large communities of slaves in a culture where the plantation was a cornerstone of local society.

Some may find the descriptions of slavery compiled within these pages to be puzzling. Many of the men and women are frank about the harsh conditions they lived under during slavery, but just as many appear to look back upon their experiences as slaves with a sense of nostalgia. James Bolton embodies that sentiment when he says, "Now I going to tell you the truth. Now that it's all over, I don't find life so good in my old age as it was in slavery when I was chillun down on Marster's plantation."

Readers should bear in mind that the interviews were conducted in the late 1930s, during one of our nation's darkest hours. By that time, even the youngest of those born into slavery were well into their seventies, and most were much older. What were already long, hard lives were undoubtedly made even harder by the one-two punch of old age and a nationwide economic depression. Add to that the nostalgia most of us feel for childhood and it is perhaps easier to understand why these former slaves could view their days under slavery as pleasurable, even joyful, periods of their lives.

The context of the interviews should also be considered when reading these accounts. The interviews were conducted primarily by whites, in a culture where blacks were often taught to tell those in authority what they wanted to hear. The most virulent antislavery members of the black community would have probably fled to the North at the first opportunity; at the very least, they would not have made themselves available for the interviews. Those who did consent quite possibly recounted only what they thought their interviewers wanted them to say.

To be certain, the inner voices of these men and women are not always readily apparent on the surface of their words. Readers of this collection will quickly recognize a pattern in the narratives. In almost all cases, the narratives begin with a recitation of the plantation or county where the interviewees were slaves and the names of their masters. From there, the accounts progress to the mundane details of slave life: who did the cooking, how clothes were provided, who tended the children, what food was served. As the narratives progress, they typically delve into aspects of the slaves' social life: church, corn shuckings, meals, weddings, and funerals. This pattern is by design. Field workers were given a list of questions to ask the former slaves, and few deviated from the list. One of my disappointments with the narratives is that the interviewers didn't stray from this predetermined list more often, as it seems that untold riches could have been gathered had the former slaves been encouraged to recollect freely. But we must remember that the interviewers were simply performing their duties as instructed. They had much work to do and could only devote so much time to each interview.

Despite these caveats, I believe there is much wealth in the narratives. The words light fire, gaining a sense of excitement and urgency, when the former slaves strike upon an important story to tell or are compelled to impart a hard-earned bit of wisdom. Tales of wedding, funerals, and encounters with the Union army have a particular energy. At those moments, sociological influences step aside, as do the mundane routines of life, and the human voice shines through.

Following the lead of Belinda Hurmence, I have chosen to include only narratives written in the first-person. There are many wonderful narratives written in the third-person, containing much valuable information. However, for the purpose of this collection, which hopes to serve as an introduction to the slave narratives, I felt that third-person material lacked the intimacy of the first-person narratives. The true appeal of the slave narratives, I believe, is being "talked to" by voices from the past.

I gathered the material in this collection from a variety of sources. The slave narratives at the Library of Congress—the narratives submitted to the library by the Federal Writers' Project in the late 1930s and early 1940s—serve as the foundation. However, I have also included several narratives that were stored in the library at the University of Georgia and were not included in the original Library of Congress material; the reason why that material was never submitted to Washington, D.C., has been lost to time. I have also included the narratives of two former Georgia slaves that I found in the WPA Life Histories Collection. Another remarkable feat of the Federal Writers' Project, this collection contains over twenty-nine hundred documents from twenty-four states. It covers all aspects of Depression-era life for whites, blacks, men, women, rich, and poor and is fascinating reading in itself. I am grateful to have stumbled upon it in the course of my research.

In assembling these narratives, I have included approximately equal numbers of men and women. At first, this was simply an attempt to balance the collection, but it soon became clear that the experiences of men and women under slavery often varied greatly. I also tried to balance the narratives by geographical region. In this effort, however, I was much less successful. I found that many of the narratives came from the Athens and Augusta areas. I was frustrated in my effort to find narratives from the coastal areas of Georgia and from urban areas such as Savannah and Atlanta.

In many of the narratives, the men and women spend as much time describing their lives after slavery as during it. This is not surprising, since most were only small children when slavery ended and had the majority of their lives before them. I struggled with these postslavery accounts, realizing that the book was intended to be a firsthand account of the lives of slaves. Ultimately, however, I decided that editing the postslavery material out of the book would have been an injustice to the lives of these men and women. I point to the narrative of the ex-slave of J. H. Hill—the only one in the collection where the interviewee's name was not recorded—as an example of the amazing information that would have been lost had I decided to include only material from slavery times. After he gained his freedom, this remarkable man went on to lead a successful life as a mason in Atlanta. He provides a fascinating look at the rebuilding of a Southern city.

Dialect posed another problem. The writers and

editors of the Federal Writers' Project took great pains to capture the slaves' vernacular on the page, often with mixed results. While editing the narratives, I was aware that the heavy use of dialect might cause modern readers to stumble, because I often struggled to interpret the words myself. I did not want unusual spellings and abbreviations to lessen the effect of the narratives, nor did I want to alter the words in any way. Ultimately, I struck upon a compromise, correcting the more obscure abbreviations and misspellings the interviewers used for dialect. I cut a small amount of repetitive material and occasionally rearranged material in the proper sequence. Brackets are employed throughout the narratives to interpret or clarify obscure words and references; many of these brackets were supplied by the interviewers themselves, although I also employed this device myself when I felt it was necessary.

I assure readers that this editing has done nothing to alter the slaves' words or, more importantly, their voices. The joy and the fear, the bitterness, hate, love, and happiness in this collection belong only to the men and women who uttered the words. What is remarkable is that they still speak so clearly to us today, warning us of the horrors of human bondage and describing the crimes in our nation's history at the same time they remind us of the emotions we all share. Their voices touch us, leaving us enriched for having listened.

On Jordan's Stormy Banks

Neal Upson

Age 81 when interviewed
in Athens, Georgia, in 1938

I WAS BORNED on Marster Frank Upson's place down in Oglethorpe County, nigh Lexington, Georgia. Marster had a plantation, but us never lived there, for us stayed at the homeplace, what never had more than 'bout eighty acres of land round it. Us never had to trot to the store every time us started to cook, 'cause what wasn't raised on the homeplace Marster had 'em raise out on the big plantation. Everything us needed to eat and wear was growed on Marse Frank's land.

Harold and Jane Upson was my daddy and mammy, only folks just called Daddy "Hal." Both of 'em was raised right on the Upson place, where they played together while they was chillun. Mammy said she had washed and sewed for Daddy ever since she was big enough, and when they got grown they just up and got married. I was their only boy, and I was the baby chile, but they had four gals older than me. They was Cordelia, Anne, Parthene, and Ella. Ella was named for Marse Frank's only chile, little Miss Ellen, and our little miss was sho' a good little chile.

Daddy made the shoes for all the slaves on the plantation, and Mammy was called the house woman. She done the cookin' up at the big house and made the cloth for her own family's clothes, and she was so smart us always had plenty to eat and wear. I was little and stayed with Mammy up at the big house and just played all over it, and all the folks up there petted me. Aunt Tama was a old slave, too old to work. She was all the time cookin' gingerbread and hidin' it in a little trunk what set by the fireplace in her room. When us chillun was good, Aunt Tama give us gingerbread, but if us didn't mind what she said us didn't get none. Aunt Tama had the rheumatiz and walked with a stick, and I could get in that trunk just about anytime I wanted to. I sho' did get 'bout everything them other chillun had, swappin' Aunt Tama's gingerbread. When our white folks went off, Aunt Tama toted the keys, and she evermore did make them niggers stand round. Marse Frank just laughed when they made complaints 'bout her.

In summertime, they cooked peas and other vegetables for us chillun in a wash pot out in the yard in the shade, and us ate out of the pot with our wooden spoons. They just give us wooden bowls full of bread and milk for supper.

Marse Frank said he wanted 'em to learn me how to wait on the white folks' table up at the big house, and they started me off with the job of fannin' the flies away. Mist'ess Serena, Marse Frank's wife, made me a white coat to wear in the dinin' room. That little old white coat made me get the only whuppin' Marse Frank ever did give me. Us had company for dinner that day, and I felt so big showin' off for 'em in that white coat that I just couldn't make that turkey wing fan do right. Them turkey wings was fastened on long handles, and after Marster had done warned me a time or two to mind what I was 'bout, the old turkey wing went down in the gravy bowl, and when I jerked it out it splattered all over the preacher's best Sunday suit. Marse Frank got up and took me right out to the kitchen, and when he got through brushin' me off I never did have no more trouble with them turkey wings.

Everybody cooked on open fireplaces them days. They had swingin' racks what they called cranes to hang the pots on for boilin'. There was ovens for bakin', and the heavy iron skillets had long handles. One of them old skillets was so big that Mammy could cook thirty biscuits in it at one time. I always did love biscuits, and I would go out in the yard and trade Aunt Tama's gingerbread to the other chillun for their share of biscuits. Then they would be scared to eat the gingerbread 'cause I told 'em I'd tell on 'em. Aunt Tama thought they was sick and told Marse Frank the chillun weren't eatin' nothin'. He asked 'em what was the matter, and they told him they had done traded all their bread to me.

Marse Frank then asked me if I weren't gettin' enough to eat, 'cause he 'lowed there was enough there for all. Then Aunt Tama had to go and tell on me. She said I was worse then a hog after them biscuits, so our good marster ordered her to see that little Neal had enough to eat.

I ain't never going to forget that whuppin' my own daddy give me. He had just sharpened up a fine new ax for himself, and I traded it off to a white boy name Roar what lived nigh us when I seed him out tryin' to cut wood with a sorry old dull ax. I sold him my daddy's fine new ax for five biscuits. When he found out 'bout that, he 'lowed he was going to give me somethin' to make me think 'fore I done any more tradin' of his things. Let me tell you, that beatin' he give me ever-more was a-layin' on of the rod.

One day, Miss Serena put me in the cherry tree to pick cherries for her, and she told me not to eat none 'til I finished; then I could have all I wanted. But I didn't mind her, and I ate so many cherries I got sick and fell out of the tree. Mist'ess was scared, but Marse Frank said, "It's good enough for him, 'cause he didn't mind."

Mammy never did give me but one whuppin' nei-ther. Daddy was going to the circus, and I just cut up 'bout it 'cause I wanted to go so bad. Mist'ess give me some cake, and I hushed long as I was eatin', but soon as the last cake crumb was swallowed I started bawlin' again. She give me a stick of candy, and soon as I ate that I was squallin' worse than ever. Mammy told

Mist'ess then that she knew how to quiet me, and she reached under the bed for a shoe. When she had done finished layin' that shoe on me and put it back where she got it, I was sure willin' to shut my mouth and let 'em all go to the circus without no more racket from me.

The first school I went to was in a little one-room house in our white folks' backyard. Us had a white teacher, and all they learned slave chillun was just plain readin' and writin'. I had to pass Dr. Willingham's office lots, and he was all the time pesterin' me about spellin'. One day, he stopped me and asked me if I could spell "bumblebee without its tail," and he said that when I learned to spell it he would give me some candy.

Mr. Sanders at Lexington give me a dime once. It was the first money I ever had. I was plumb rich, and I never let my daddy have no piece 'til he fetched me to town to do my tradin'. I was all set to buy myself a hat, a store-bought suit of clothes, and some shoes what weren't brogans, but I wound up with a ginger cake and a nickel's worth of candy.

I used to cry and holler every time Miss Serena went off and left me. Whenever I seen 'em gettin' out the carriage to hitch it up, I started beggin' to go. Sometimes she laughed and said, "All right, Neal." But when she said, "No, Neal," I snuck out and hid under the high-up carriage seat and went along just the same. Mist'ess always found me 'fore us got back home, but she just laughed and said, "Well, Neal's my little nigger anyhow."

Marster had one of them old cotton gins what didn't have no engines. It was worked by mules. Them old mules was hitched to a long pole what they pulled round and round to make the gin do its work. They had some gins in them days what had treadmills for the mules to walk in. Them old treadmills looked sort of like stairs, but most of 'em was turned by long poles what the mules pulled. You had to feed the cotton by hand to them old gins, and you sure had to be careful or you was going to lose a hand and maybe a arm. You had to jump in them old cotton presses and feed the cotton down by hand. It took 'most all day long to gin two bales of cotton, and if there was three bales to be ginned us had to work 'most all night to finish up.

They mixed wool with the lint cotton to spin thread to make cloth for our winter clothes. Mammy wove a lot of that cloth, and the clothes made out of it sure would keep out the cold. Most of our stockin's and socks was knit at home, but now and then somebody would get hold of a store-bought pair for Sunday-go-to-meetin' wear.

Colored folks went to church with their own white folks and sat in the gallery. One Sunday, us was all settin' in that church listenin' to the white preacher, Mr. Hansford, tellin' how the old devil was going to get them what didn't do right. A nigger had done run off from his marster and was hidin' out from one place to another. At night, he would go steal somethin' to eat. He had done stole some chickens and had 'em with him up in the church steeple, where he was hidin' that day. When daytime come, he went off to sleep like niggers do when they ain't got to hustle, and when he woke up, Preacher Hansford was tellin' 'em 'bout how the devil was going to get the sinners. Right then, an old rooster what he had stole up crowed so loud it seemed like Gabriel's trumpet on Judgment Day. That runaway nigger was scared 'cause he knowed they was going to find him sure, but he weren't scared nothin' compared to them niggers settin' in the gallery. They just knowed that was the voice of the devil what had come after 'em. Them niggers never stopped prayin' and testifyin' to the Lord 'til the white folks had done got that runaway slave and the rooster out of the steeple. His marster was there and took him home and gave him a good, sound thrashin'.

Slaves was allowed to have prayer meetin' on Tuesday and Friday round at the different plantations where their marsters didn't care, and there weren't many what objected. The good marsters all give their slaves prayer meetin' passes on them nights so the patterollers wouldn't get 'em and beat 'em up for bein' off their marsters' lands. They 'most nigh killed some slaves what they catch out when they didn't have no pass. White preachers done the talkin' at the meetin' houses, but at them Tuesday- and Friday-night prayer meetin's it was all done by niggers. I was too little to 'member much 'bout them meetin's, but my older sisters used to talk lots 'bout 'em long after the war had brung our Freedom. There weren't many slaves what could read, so they jus' talked 'bout what they done heard the white preachers say on Sunday. One of the favorite texts was the third chapter from John, and most of 'em just 'membered a line or two from that. From what folks said 'bout them meetin's, there was sure a lot of good prayin' and testifyin', 'cause so many sinners repented and was saved.

Sometimes at them Sunday meetin's at the white folks' church, they would have two or three preachers the same day. The first one would give the text and preach for at least a hour, then another would give a text and do his preachin', and 'bout that time another one would rise up and say that them first brothers had done preached enough to save three thousand soul, but that he was going to try to double that number. Then he would do his preachin', and after that one of them others would get up and say, "Brothers and sisters, us is all here for the same and only purpose—that of savin' souls. These other good brothers is done preached, talked and prayed and let the gap down; now I'm going to raise it. Us is going to get religion enough to take us straight through them pearly gates."

When old Aunt Flora come up and wanted to join the church, she told 'bout how she had done seen the heavenly light and changed her way of livin'. Folks testified then 'bout the goodness of the Lord and His many blessin's what He give to saints and sinners. Them days, they examined folks 'fore they let 'em join up with the church. When they started examinin' Aunt Flora, the preacher asked her, "Is you done been borned again, and does you believe that Jesus Christ done died to save sinners?" Aunt Flora, she started to cry, and she said, "Lordy, is He dead? Us didn't know that. If my old man had done 'scribed for the paper like I told him to, us would have knowed when Jesus died."

Them days, it was the custom for marsters to hire out what slaves they had that weren't needed to work on their own land, so our marster hired out two of my sisters. Sis' Anna was hired to a family 'bout sixteen miles from our place. She didn't like it there so she run away, and I found her hid out in our tater house. One day when us was playin', she called to me right low and soft like and told me she was hungry and for me to get her somethin' to eat but not to tell nobody she was there. She said she had been there with nothin' to eat for several days. She was scared Marster might whip her. She looked so thin and bad I thought she was going to die, so I told Mammy. Her and Marster went and brung Anna to the house and fed her. That poor child was starved 'most to death. Marster kept her at home for three weeks and fed her up good, then he carried her back and told them folks what had hired her that they had better treat Anna good and see that she had plenty to eat. Marster was drivin' a fast hoss that day, but Anna beat him back home that day. She cried and took on so, beggin' him not to take her back there no more, that he told her she could stay home. My other sister stayed on where she was hired out 'til the war was over and they give us our Freedom.

Daddy had done hid all old Marster's hosses when the Yankees got to our plantation. Two of the ridin' hosses was in the smokehouse, and another good trotter was in the henhouse. Old Jake was a slave what wasn't right bright. He slept in the kitchen, and he knowed where Daddy had hid them hosses, but that was all he knowed. Marster had given Daddy his money to hide, too, and he took some of the plasterin' off the wall in Marster's room and put the box of money inside the wall. Then he fixed that plasterin' back so nice you couldn't tell it had ever been tore off.

The night them Yankees come, Daddy had gone out to the workhouse to get some pegs to fix somethin'— us didn't have no nails in them days. When the Yankees rid up to the kitchen door and found old Jake right by hisself, that poor old fool was scared so bad he just started right off babblin' 'bout two hosses in the smokehouse and one in the henhouse, but he was tremblin' so he couldn't talk plain. Old Marster heard the fuss they made, and he come down to the kitchen to see what was the matter. The Yankees then ordered Marster to get 'em his hosses. Marster called Daddy and told him to get the hosses, but Daddy, he played foolish like and stalled round like he didn't have good sense. Them soldiers raved and fussed all night long 'bout them hosses, but they never thought 'bout lookin' in the smokehouse and the henhouse for 'em, and 'bout daybreak they left without takin' a thing. Marster said he was sure proud of my daddy for savin' them good hosses for him.

Mammy died 'bout a year after the war, and I never will forget how Mist'ess cried and said, "Neal, your mammy is done gone, and I don't know what I'll do without her."

Not long after that, Daddy bid for the contract to carry the mail, and he got the place, but it made the white folks right mad, 'cause some white folks had put in bids for that contract. They 'lowed that Daddy better not start out with the mail, 'cause if he did he was going to be sorry. Marster begged Daddy not to risk it and told him if he would stay there with him he would let him have a plantation for as long as he lived, and so us stayed on there 'til Daddy died, and a long time after that us kept on workin' for old Marster.

When the war was over, they closed the little one-room school what our good marster had kept in his backyard for his slaves, but our young Miss Ellen learned my sister right on 'til she got where she could teach school. Daddy fixed up a room on to our house for her school, and she soon had it full of chillun. They made me study, too, and I sure did hate to have to go to school to my own sister, for she evermore did take every chance to lay that stick on me, but I suspects she had a right tough time with me. When time come round to celebrate school commencement, I was one proud little nigger 'cause I never had been so dressed up in my life before. I had on a red waist, white pants, and a good pair of shoes, but the grandest thing of all 'bout that outfit was Daddy let me wear his watch. Everybody came for that celebration. There was over three hundred folks at that big dinner, and us had lots of barbecue and all sorts of good things to eat. Old Marster was there, and when I stood up 'fore all them folks and said my little speech without missin' a word, Marster sure did laugh and clap his hands. He called me over to where he was settin' and said, "I knowed you could learn if you wanted to." Best of all, he give me a whole dollar. I was rich then, plumb rich. One of my sisters couldn't learn nothin'. The only letters she could ever say was "G-O-D." No matter what you asked her to spell, she always said, "G-O-D." She was a good field hand, though, and a good woman, and she lived to be more than eighty years old.

Now, talkin' 'bout frolickin', us really used to dance. What I means is sure-'nough old-time breakdowns. Sometimes us didn't have no music 'cept just beatin' time on tin pans and buckets, but most times old Edice Hudson played his fiddle for us, and it had to be tuned again after every set us danced. He never knowed but one tune, and he played that over and over. Sometimes there was ten or eleven couples on the floor at the same time, and us didn't think nothin' of dancin' all night long. Us had plenty of old corn juice for refreshment, and after Edice had two or three cups of that juice he could get "Turkey in the Straw" out of that fiddle like nobody's business.

One time, a houseboy from another plantation wanted to come to one of our Saturday-night dances, so his marster told him to shine his boots for Sunday and fix his hoss for the night, and then he could get off for the frolic. Abraham shined his marster's boots 'til he could see himself in 'em, and they looked so grand he was tempted to try 'em on. They was a little tight, but he thought he could wear 'em, and he wanted to show hisself off in 'em at the dance. They weren't so easy to walk in, and he was 'fraid he might get 'em scratched up walkin' through the fields, so he snuck his marster's hoss out and rode to the dance. When Abraham ride up there in them shiny boots, he got all the gals' 'tention. None of 'em wanted to dance with the other niggers. That Abraham was sure struttin', 'til somebody run in and told him his hoss had done broke its neck. He had tied it to a limb, and sure 'nough, some way, that hoss had done got tangled up and hung its own self. Abraham begged the other nigger boys to help him take the dead hoss home, but he had done took their gals, and he didn't get no help. He had to walk twelve long miles home in them tight shoes.

The sun had done risen up when he got there, and it wasn't long 'fore his marster was callin', "Abraham, bring me my boots." That nigger would holler out, "Yes, sir! I'm a-comin'." But them boots wouldn't come off 'cause his feet had swelled up in 'em. His marster kept callin', and when Abraham saw he couldn't put it off no longer he just cut them boots off his feet and went in and told what he had done. His marster was awful mad and said he was of a good mind to take the hide off Abraham's back. "Go get my hoss quick, nigger, 'fore I kill you!" he yelled. Then Abraham told him, "Marster, I know you is going to kill me now, but your hoss is dead." Then poor Abraham had to cut and tell the whole story, and his marster got to laughin' so 'bout how he took all the gals away from the other boys and how them boots hurt him that it looked like he never would stop. When he finally did stop laughin' and shakin' his sides, he said, "That's all right, Abraham. Don't never let nobody beat your time with the gals." And that's all he ever said to Abraham about it.

My daddy and his cousin Jim swore with one another that if one died 'fore the other that the one what was left would look after the dead one's family and see that none of the chillun was bound out to work for nobody. It wasn't long after this that Daddy died. I was just fourteen and was workin' for a brick mason, learnin' that trade. Daddy had done been sick awhile, and one night the family woke me up and said he was dyin'. I run fast as I could for a doctor, but Daddy was dead when I got back. Us buried him right 'side of Mammy in the old graveyard. It was 'most a year after that 'fore us had the funeral sermon preached. That was the way folks done then.

Now Mammy and Daddy was both gone, but old Marster said us chillun could live there long as us wanted to. I went on back to work, 'cause I was crazy to be as good a mason as my daddy was. In Lexington, there is a rock wall still standin' round a whole square what Daddy built in slavery time.

Long as he lived, he blowed his bugle every mornin' to wake up all the folks on Marse Frank's plantation. He never failed to blow that bugle at break of day 'cept on Sundays, and everybody on that place depended on him to wake 'em up.

I was just a-workin' away one day when Cousin Jim sent for me to go to town with him. That man brung me right here to Athens to the old courthouse and bound me out to a white man. He done that very thing after swearin' to my daddy he wouldn't never let that happen. I didn't want to work that way, so I run away and went back home to work. The sheriff came and got me and said I had to go back where I was bound out or go to jail. Pretty soon, I run away again and went to Atlanta, and they never bothered me 'bout that no more.

I farmed with the white folks for thirty-two years and never had no trouble with nobody. Us always settled up fair and square, and in crop time they never bothered to come round to see what Neal was doin', 'cause they knowed this nigger was working all right. They was all mighty good to me. After I got so old I couldn't run a farm no more, I worked in the white folks' gardens and tended their flowers.

I done been married two times, but it was the first time that was the sure-'nough excitin' one. I courted that gal for a long, long time while I was too scared to ask her daddy for her. I went to see her every Sunday just determined to ask him for her 'fore I left, and I would stay late after supper but just couldn't get up nerve enough to do it. One Sunday, I promised myself I would ask him if it killed me, so I went over to his house early that mornin' and told Lida—that was my sweetheart's name—I says to her, "I sure is going to ask him today."

Well, dinnertime come, suppertime come, and I was gettin' shaky in my joints when her daddy went to feed his hogs, and I went along with him. This is the way I finally did ask him for his gal. He said he was goin' to have some fine meat come winter. I asked him if it would be enough for all of his family, and he said, "How come you ask that, boy?" Then I just got a tight hold on that old hogpen and said, "Well, sir, I just thought that if you didn't have enough for all of 'em, I could take Lida." I felt myself goin' down. He started laughin' fit to kill. "Boy," he says, "is you tryin' to ask for Lida? If so, I don't care 'cause she's got to get married sometime." I was so happy I left him right then and run back to tell Lida that he said it was all right.

Us didn't have no big weddin'. Lida had on a new calico dress, and I wore new jeans pants. Marster heard us was gettin' married that day, and he sent his new buggy with a message for us to come right back there to him. I told Lida us better go, so us got in that buggy and drive off, and the rest of the folks followed in the wagon. Marster met us in front of old Salem Church. He had the church open and Preacher John Gibson waitin' there to marry us. Us weren't expectin' no church weddin', but Marster said that Neal had to get married right. He never did forget his niggers.

Lida, she's been dead a long time, and I married again, but that wasn't like the first time.

Mollie Kinsey
Age 84
when interviewed in 1939

YOU SAY YOU WANT me to talk to you 'bout the experience of my life—is this something 'bout *Gone With the Wind*? Oh, I thought maybe it was. I've heard so much about the premieres of *Gone With the Wind* I just knowed when you asked me to talk with you it was something 'bout that. Well, that's all right. I wouldn't have minded telling you nohow if it was, for I got a record, and I don't mind telling it to nobody.

I was ten years old when set free, and I was set free with a blind ma. They sold my father in 1858. I never 'member seeing him. See, I was three years old, and I don't 'member him. They sold him from Ma and five chillun.

My home life was 'bout like the ordinary chile's in them days, and I guess I was 'bout like the chillun is today. All I can say, I was just a little bad gal. Course, I was never a very small girl in stature, was very large, and when I was only a small girl people always called me "woman" because of my size. I don't 'spect I was no different to the chillun today, for I notice they do 'bout the same things I did when I was a chile.

I was born and raised in Washington, Georgia, right in town, and I never saw the country or cotton grow 'til I was 'bout grown.

My father used to belong to Mr. Sam Ellington. He sold him to Dick Petite, a speculator from Mississippi. I don't 'member it, but Ma told us chillun 'bout it when we growed up.

They had slaves in pens—brung in droves and put in them pens, just like they was cows. They sold them by auctioning off to the highest bidder. I was only a chile and never went round much. They put girls on the block and auctioned them off: "What will you give for this nigger wench?" Lots of the girls was sold by their master who was their father, taken right out of the yards with their white chillun and sold like herds of cattle.

My sister was given away when she was a girl. She told me and Ma that they'd make her go out and lay on a table, and two or three white men would have innercourse with her before they'd let her get up. She was just a small girl. She died when she was still in her young days, still a girl. Oh! You is blessed to live in this day and don't know the tortures the slaves went through. Honey, slavery was bad, but I was so young I missed all the evil. But chile, I knowed 'bout it.

My master whipped me once, and he never just whipped me for nothing. It was something I'd done. I was scared of him, too. I see chillun doing things they shouldn't do, but I can't say nothing, for I was a chile and did the same thing once. I got a lot of whippings from my ma, for I was a bad chile. My master would tell me to do a job, and I would do it willingly, but I went 'bout it slow like, and he'd holler, "Concarn it, get a move on you!" I'd say, "I make haste, Marse George, I make haste."

My ma's first owner was Marse Hamilton, and he give her away to Marse Dison. Then Marse Dison give Ma and us chillun to Marse George. I was born in Washington, Georgia, on February 28, 1855, and when I was set free with a blind ma, she took me to Sparta, Georgia. I had to work hard, for with a blind ma it was nothing she could do to earn money. I didn't have nobody to help me but Ma's brother. I'd go to him to get a little something for food. I stayed in Sparta until 1928. I got lots of work there.

I married in Sparta and was very happy. My husband took care of me, and life wasn't so hard. He died, and in a year or so after that I married again. My first husband was good to my blind ma, and when she died he come home from work to stay with me and console me. He was a good Christian man. My first husband drove a carriage for drummers round through the country. He loved me. He supported me and our chillun and my blind ma. The white folks he worked for liked him, and they was nice to me, too. After my husband's death, I worked and made a good living. I cooked, washed, ironed for the white folks. When I married my second husband, I sho' married a wealthy man. I 'member I went into the smokehouse, and when I saw all that meat, hams, shoulders, lard, and sausage in that house, I said, "Lawdy, is all this mine?" He had turkeys, geese, guinea, and ducks.

After my husband Mr. Kinsey died, I opened a restaurant in Sparta, and I didn't run no shoddy place either. The best people ate at my place. Mr. Britt, a businessman there in Sparta, and for whose wife I'd nursed, would tell people to go down to eat at Mollie's Place. I fed white and colored. I had a place in the front where I served the white, and they liked my vittles, too. Soldiers, railroad men, and drummers come to eat at my place. I stayed in Sparta until 1928, when times got so bad.

I joined the A.M.E. Church in 1871. I crossed over on the Lord's side then and have been there ever since, and I'm so proud of it.

Did I tell you that God called me to preach? Well, he did in 1914. I was in Sparta, in my restaurant, and I was tired. I went out on the front steps and sat down. While I sat there, I saw a young boy that I knowed since he was a baby in his ma's arms, and [he was with] some more mens in stripes, chained together, from the chain gang. I sat there, my heart bleeding for that boy. My heart was so heavy, and I had so much sorrow in my heart for him, and I prayed for him. I couldn't get him off my mind. I went home that night and read my Bible, honey. I got with the Lord. I turned page after page and read. I got down on my knees and prayed. I said, "God, I don't want to go to the chain gang, and I don't want to go to hell. I want to be your servant. Take me and use me as you will." That morning, just before day, I had a call. God Almighty put a seal on my right hand—this hand—and he lifted me in an airplane and carried me through the sky and landed me down in my churchyard. I was preaching, preaching, telling what God had done and of his blessings. When I landed in the churchyard, some of my sisters and brothers of the church was there. Some of the sisters said, "Here you come with a new religion." I told them, "No, this is the same old-time religion." And God had called me to preach, to go out and tell the world of his great love, and I was preaching and was going to do service for Him. He had put a seal on my hand, marking me for His cause.

I didn't go out and preach on the highways and byways, but I tell you I preached, and I'm still preaching. I'm preaching in my home.

I've stayed in the A.M.E. Church since I was sixteen years old. Both of my husbands was Baptist, but I stayed in the A.M.E. Church. Some people have gone from church to church, but I stayed in the faith, and

I'm going to heaven someday. I'm going to put on my robe, my crown, my golden slippers, and [I'm] going to heaven. I'm going to walk them golden streets, and I ain't going to study war no more. Honey, I has fought a battle here.

Male ex-slave of
Senator J. H. Hill
*Interviewed
in his home in Atlanta*

MY PARENTS WERE SLAVES on the plantation of John H. Hill, a slave owner in Madison, Georgia. I was born May 21, 1855. I was owned and kept by J. H. Hill until just before surrender. I was a small boy when Sherman left here at the fall of Atlanta. He came through Madison on his March to the Sea, and we chillun hung out on the front fence from early morning 'til late in the evening, watching the soldiers go by. It took most of the day.

My master was a senator from Georgia, elected on the Whig ticket. He served two terms in Washington as senator. His wife, our mistress, had charge of the slaves and plantation. She never seemed to like the idea of having slaves. Of course, I never heard her say she didn't want them, but she was the one to free the slaves on the place before surrender. Since that time, I've felt she didn't want them in the first place.

The next week after Sherman passed through Madison, Miss Emily called the five women that was on the place and told them to stay round the house and attend to things as they had always done, until their husbands come back. She said they were free and could go wherever they wanted to. See, she decided this before surrender and told them they could keep up just as before, until their husbands could look after a place for them to stay. She meant that they could rent from her if they wanted to. In that number of women was my mother, Ellen, who worked as a seamstress for Mrs. Hill. The other women was Aunt Lizzie and Aunt Dina, the washerwomen, Aunt Liza, a seamstress to help my mother, and Aunt Caroline, the nurse for Miss Emily's chillun.

I never worked as a slave because I wasn't old enough. In 1864, when I was nine years old, they sent me on a trial visit to the plantation to give me an idea of what I had to do someday. The place I'm talking about, when I was sent for the tryout, was on the outskirts of town. It was a house where they sent chillun out old enough to work for a sort of training. I guess you'd call it the training period. When the chillun was near ten years old, they had this week's trial to get them used to the work they'd have to do when they reached ten years. At the age of ten, they was then sent to the field to work. They'd chop, hoe, pick cotton, and pull fodder, corn, or anything else to be done on the plantation. I stayed at the place a whole week and was brought home on Saturday. That week's work showed me what I was to do when I was ten years old. Well, this was just before Sherman's march from Atlanta to the sea, and I never got a chance to go to the plantation to work again, for Miss Emily freed all on her place, and soon after we was emancipated.

The soldiers I mentioned awhile ago that passed with Sherman carried provisions, hams, shoulders, meal, flour, and other food. They had their cooks and their servants. I 'member seeing a woman in that crowd of servants. She had a baby in her arms. She hollered at us chillun and said, "You chillun get off that fence and go learn your ABC's." I thought she was crazy telling us that, for we had never been 'lowed to learn nothing at all like reading and writing. I learned, but it was after surrender, and I was over ten years old.

It was soon after the soldiers passed with Sherman that Miss Emily called in all the women servants and told them they could take their chillun to the cabin and stay there until after the war. My father, George, had gone with Josh Hill, a son of Miss Emily's, to wait on him. She told my mother to take us to that cabin until a place could be made for us.

I said I was born a slave, but I was too young to know much about slavery. I was the property of the

Hill family from 1855 to 1865, when Freedom was declared and they said we was free.

My master had four sons. Three of them went to the army. Legree Hill, the youngest son, went to the war at the age of eighteen years. He was killed in the Kennesaw Mountains. His mother seemed sad over his going because he was too young and ran off and went. A sharpshooter killed him. His father went for him. He was buried in the Yankee line, wrapped in a blanket. He had some of the money he had when he was killed on him. He was dressed like a Yankee, in their uniform. Of course, nothing much was said about it, as I 'member, 'cause he wasn't supposed to be a Yankee at all. He was fighting against the Yankees. When he was stirred up to go to the war, he told his mother that he wanted to go because he wanted to bring Lincoln's head back, and he was going after his head. He didn't get to come back. Another son, Clarence, a cavalryman, was the oldest son. He had two horses shot out from under him, but he escaped himself.

I left Madison and went to Athens, Georgia. I learned the trade of brick masonry and plastering. I moved to Athens on the second of April in 1877. I went there to work for a contractor, Nasus McGinty. I stayed in Athens from April 1877 until August 1880. I then moved to Atlanta. This was the beginning of life for me in Atlanta. I have been here ever since, working at my trade, except for short intervals when I went out to work, out of town.

I built this house in 1887 and moved in the same year on December 27. At first, it only had ten or twelve rooms. My house now is somewhat larger than Colonel Hill's house, where the family lived who owned us as slaves.

I've seen Atlanta grow from a town of woods, pig and cow paths, to a great city of paved streets, tall buildings, and beautifully lighted streets. You wouldn't believe it, but there was creeks and branches running along where the main part of town is now. There is a creek under the First National Bank Building, and I 'member when they was building that bank they got a alligator out of the creek. It was small, as I recall now, but 'magine that all along where the fine buildings is now. And to think I've lived to see all of this growth.

I've witnessed some trying times here, too. I saw the riot and the great fire that practically burned up a part of Atlanta. I saw the toll of the riot—hatred, prejudice, and murder. I was working out on what is now Highland Avenue at the time. Soldiers had to be sent out, and they was supposed to protect everyone, but some of them didn't uphold the law. There was a gang of soldiers, and I say *gang* because that is just what I feel they was, from the way they acted. Dressed in uniform of Uncle Sam and sent out because they was supposed to keep the law, and there they was breaking it. They was acting like ordinary, revengeful people, pouring out their hatred for the Negro. Those soldiers came down the streets shouting and singing,

"We are rough, we are tough,
We are rough, we are tough,
We will kill niggers and never get enough."

That gang of soldiers went right on marching, and when they got to McGruder Street they killed a Negro. They patrolled Randolph Street and went on down Irwin. They seemed bent on showing their wrath against the Negro. That was a pitiful time. Negroes was shot down without any cause, and they was scared to be seen on the street. We had no one, it seemed, on our side, for there was the soldiers shouting and singing. There they was really adding to the riot—more hatred, deaths, and not doing what they was supposed to do.

At the time of the riot, they claimed that only one white man was killed and thirteen Negroes. But it was rumored here—I don't know it to be true and don't know whether I ought to repeat it, but it was said the white undertaker shops was filled with victims of the riot, and they was burying them at night so the Negroes wouldn't know how many was killed. We had now way of knowing whether this was true or not. There was a man in South Atlanta who, it is said, killed two or three white men before he was captured. Really, he wasn't caught, for he barred himself in a house and shot everyone who came near the house, and the only way they got him was to burn the house, and he was burned up in it.

The same year that McKinley came through here as president, they burned a Negro, Hogue Smith. The

Georgian newspaper wasn't called the *Georgian* then, but the editor of what is now the *Georgian* ran a excursion down to Fairburn to see the burning of that Negro. That was something awful.

Well, I'm glad I've lived to see better understanding between the two races, and I do believe in not many years to come there will be no more lynchings of the Negroes, and people just like us going to witness them like as though they were places of amusement.

Sally Brown
Age 87
when interviewed in 1939

I WAS BORN FOUR MILES from Commerce, Georgia, and was thirteen years old at surrender. My mama belonged to the Nash family—three old maid sisters—and my papa belonged to General Burns, who was an officer in the war. There was six of us chillun: Lucy, Melvina, Johnnie, Callie, Joe, and me. We didn't stay together long. I was give away when I was just a baby, and I never did see my mama again. The Nashes didn't believe in sellin' slaves. If they got rid of any, it was givin' 'em away. They sold one once 'cause the other slaves said they was gonna kill him, 'cause he had a baby by his own daughter. So to keep him from being killed, they sold him.

I was give to the Mitchell family, and they done everything mean to me they could. I was put to work in the fields when I was five year old, pickin' cotton and hoein'. And I slept on the floor nine years, winter and summer, sick or well. I never wore nothin' but a cotton dress and my shimmy and drawers. I had such a hard time. That Mistress Mitchell didn't care what happened to me. Sometimes she would walk us to church, but we never went nowhere else. That woman took delight in sellin' slaves. She used to lash me with a cowhide whip. Then she died, and I went from one family to another. All the owners was pretty much the same, but this is still the Mitchell woman I'm telling you about now.

They didn't mind slaves mating, but they wanted their niggers to marry only 'mongst them on their place. They didn't allow 'em to mate with other slaves from other places. When the women had babies, they was treated kind, and they let 'em stay in. We called it "layin'," just about like they does now. We didn't go to no hospitals like they does now. We just had our babies and had a granny to catch 'em. We didn't have all the pain-easin' medicine then. The granny would put a rusty piece of tin or an ax under the straw tick, and this would ease the pains. Us didn't have no mattresses in them days, but filled a bed tick with fresh straw after the wheat was thrashed, and it was good sleepin', too. Well, the granny put a ax under my straw tick once. This was to cut off the afterpains, and it sure did, too, honey. We'd set up the fifth day, and after the layin'-in time was up we was 'lowed to walk outdoors, and they told us to walk around the house just once and come in the house. This was to keep us from takin' a lapse.

We wasn't 'lowed to go around and have pleasure as the folks does today. We had to have passes to go wherever we wanted. When we'd get out, there was a bunch of white men called the patterollers. They'd come in and see if all us had passes, and if they found any who didn't have a pass he was whipped—give fifty or mo' lashes, and they'd count them lashes. If they said a hundred, you got a hundred. They was somethin' like the Ku Klux. We was 'fraid to tell our marsters 'bout the patterollers 'cause we was scared they'd whip us again, for we was told not to tell. They'd sing a little ditty. I wish I could remember the words, but it went somethin' like this:

> "Run, nigger, run, the patterollers'll get you,
> Run, nigger, run, you'd better get away."

Slaves was treated in most cases like cattle. A man went about the country buyin' up slaves like buyin' up cattle and the like, and he was called a speculator. Then he'd sell 'em to the highest bidder. Oh! It was pitiful to see chillun took from their mothers' breast, mothers sold, husbands sold from wives. One woman he [the speculator] was to buy had a baby, and of course the baby come before he bought her, and he wouldn't buy the baby, said he hadn't bargained to buy the baby, too, and he just wouldn't. My uncle was married, but he was owned by one marster, and his wife was owned by another. He was 'lowed to visit his wife on Wednesday and Saturday; that was the earliest time he could get off. He went on Wednesday, and when he went back on Saturday his wife had been bought by the speculator, and he never did know where she was.

I worked hard always. Honey, you can't imagine what a hard time I had. I split rails like a man. How did I do it? I used a huge glut [handle] made out of wood, and an iron wedge drove into the wood with a maul, and this would split the wood.

I helped spin the cotton into thread for our clothes. The thread was wound on big branches—four branches made four outs, or one hank. After the thread was spun, we used a loom to weave the cloth. We had no sewin' machines, had to sew by hand. My mistress had a big silver bird, and she would always catch the cloth in the bird's bill, and this would hold it for her to sew.

I didn't get to handle no money when I was young. I worked from sunup to sundown. We never had overseers like some of the slaves. We was give as much work to do in a day, and if the white folks went off on a vacation they would give us so much work to do while they was gone, and we better have all of it done, too, when they'd come home.

Some of the white folks was very kind to their slaves. Some didn't believe in slavery, and some freed 'em before the war and even give 'em land and homes. Some would give the niggers meal, lard, and things like that.

They made me hoe when I was a child, and I'd keep right up with the others, 'cause they'd tell me if I got behind that a runaway nigger would get me and split open my head and get the milk out of it. Of course, I didn't know then that wasn't true. I believed everything they told me, and that made me work the harder.

There was a white man, Mr. Jim, that was very mean to the slaves. He'd go round and beat 'em. He'd even go to the little homes, tear down the chimneys and do all sorts of cruel things. The chimneys was made of mud and straw and sticks; they was powerful strong, too. Mr. Jim was just a mean man, and when he died we all said God got tired of Mr. Jim bein' so mean and killed him. When they laid him out on the coolin' board, everybody was settin' round moanin' over his death, and all of a sudden Mr. Jim rolled off the coolin' board, and such a runnin' and gettin' out of that room you never saw. We said Mr. Jim was tryin' to run the niggers, and we was 'fraid to go about at night. I believed it then. Now that there's embalmin', I know that musta been gas and he was purgin', for they didn't know nothin' 'bout embalmin' then. They didn't keep dead folks out of the ground long in them days.

Doctors wasn't so plentiful then. They'd go round in buggies and on hosses. Them that rode on a hoss had saddle pockets just filled with little bottles, and lots of 'em. He try one medicine, and if it didn't do no good he'd try another until it did good, and when the doctor went to see a sick person he'd stay right there until he was better. He didn't just come in and write a 'scription for somebody to take to a drugstore.

We used herbs a lot in them days. When a body

had dropsy, we'd set him in a tepid bath made of mullein leaves. There was a jimson weed we'd use for rheumatism, and for asthma we'd use tea made out of chestnut leaves. We'd get the chestnut leaves, dry 'em in the sun just like tea leaves, and we wouldn't let them leaves get wet for nothin' in the world while they was dryin'. We'd take poke salad roots, boil 'em, and then take sugar and make a syrup. This was the best thing for asthma; it was known to cure it, too. For colds and such, we used horehound, made candy out of it with sorghum molasses. We used a lot of rock candy and whiskey for colds, too. They had a remedy that they used for consumption—take dry cow manure, make tea of this, and flavor it with mint, and give it to the sick person. We didn't need any doctors then, for we didn't have so much sickness in them days, and naturally they didn't die so fast; folks lived a long time then. They used a lot of peach tree leaves, too, for fever, and when the stomach got upset we'd crush the leaves, pour water over 'em, and wouldn't let 'em drink any other kind of water 'til they was better. I still believes in them old homemade medicines, too, and I don't believe in so many doctors.

We didn't have stoves plentiful then, just ovens we set in the fireplace. I toted many a armful of bark— good old hickory bark to cook with. We'd bake light bread—both flour and corn. The yeast from this bread was made from hops. Coals of fire was put on top of the oven and under the bottom, too. Everything was cooked on coals from a wood fire—coffee and all.

The vittles was good in them days. We got our vegetables out of the garden in season and didn't have all the hothouse vegetables. I don't eat many vegetables now unless they come out of the garden and I know it. Well, as I said, there was racks fitted in the fireplace to put pots on. Once, there was a big pot settin' on the fire, just boilin' away with a roast in it. As the water boiled, the meat turned over and over, comin' up to the top and goin' down again. Ole Sandy, the dog, came in the kitchen. We sat there awhile and watched the meat roll over and over in the pot, and all of a sudden like he grabbed at that meat and pulls it out of the pot. Course, he couldn't eat it 'cause it was hot, and they got the meat before he ate it.

The kitchen was away from the big house, so the vittles was cooked and carried up to the house. I'd carry it up myself. We wasn't 'lowed to eat all the different kind of vittles the white folks eat. And one mornin' when I was carryin' the breakfast to the big house, we had waffles that was a pretty golden brown and pipin' hot. They was a picture to look at, and I just couldn't keep from takin' one, and that was the hardest waffle for me to eat before I got to the big house I ever saw. I just couldn't get that waffle down 'cause my conscience whipped me so.

They taught me to do everything. I used battlin' blocks and battlin' sticks to help clean the clothes when we was washin'; we all did. We took the clothes out of the suds, soaped 'em good, and put 'em on the block, and beat 'em with a battlin' stick, which was made like a paddle. On wash days, you could hear them battlin' sticks poundin' every which way. We made our own soap, used old meat and grease and poured water over wood ashes, which was kept in a racklike thing, and the water would drip through the ashes. This made strong lye. We used a lotta such lye, too, to boil with.

Sometimes the slaves would run away. Their marsters was mean to 'em and caused 'em to run away. Sometimes they'd live in caves. How'd they get along? Well, child, they got along all right, what with other people slippin' things in to 'em. And then they'd steal hogs, chickens, and anything else they could get their hands on. Some white people would help, too, for there was some white people who didn't believe in slavery. Yes, they'd try to find them slaves that run away, and if they was found they'd be beat or sold to somebody else. My grandmother run away from her marster. She used sand for soap. Yes, child, I reckon they got 'long all right in the caves. They had babies in there, and raised 'em, too.

I stayed with the Mitchells 'til Miss Hannah died. I even helped lay her out. I didn't go to the graveyard, though. I didn't have a home after she died, and I wandered from place to place, stayin' with a white family this time and then a nigger family next time. I didn't know 'bout surrender and that I was free 'til after Miss Hannah died and I got out on my own. Lots of the owners didn't tell their slaves they was freed, and so we went right on workin' like we had been befo' surrender.

I moved to Jackson County and stayed with a Mr. Frank Dowdy. I didn't stay there long, though. Then I moved to Winder, Georgia. They called it Jug Tavern in them days, 'cause jugs was made there. I married Green Hinton in Winder. Got along well after marryin' him. He farmed for a livin' and made a good livin' for me and the eight chillun, all born in Winder. The chillun was grown nearly when he died and was able to help me with the smallest ones. I got along all right after his death and didn't have such a hard time raisin' the chillun.

Then I married Jim Brown and moved to Atlanta. Jim farmed at first for a livin', and then he worked on the railroad—the Seaboard. He helped to grade the first railroad track for that line. He was a sand dryer. He was killed on the railroad. After he moved here, he bought this home. I've lived here twenty years. Jim was comin' in the railroad yard one day and stepped off the little engine they used for the workers right in the path of the L & N train. He was cut up and crushed to pieces. He didn't have a sign of a hand. They used a rake to get up the pieces they did get. A man brought a few pieces out here in a bundle, and I wouldn't even look at them. I got a little money from the railroad, but the lawyer got most of it. He brung me a few dollars out and told me not to talk about it with nobody or tell how much I got.

Times has changed so much from when I was young. You don't hear of haints as you did when I growed up. The Lord had to show His work in miracles 'cause we didn't have learnin' in them days like they has now. And you may not believe it, but them things happened. I knows an old man what died, and after his death he'd come to our house, where he always cut wood, and at night we could hear a chain bein' drug along in the yard, just as if a big log chain was bein' pulled by somebody. This went on for several nights 'til my father got tired, and one night after he heard it so long—the *chop-chop*—Papa got mad and hollered at the haint, "Goddamn you, go to hell!" and that spirit went off and never did come back.

We'd always know somebody was goin' to die when we heard a owl come to a house and start screechin'. We always said, "Somebody is going to die!" Honey, you don't hear it now, and it's good you don't, for it would scare you to death nearly. It sounded so mournful like, and we'd put the poker or the shovel in the fire, and that always run him away; it burned his tongue out, and he couldn't holler no mo'. If they'd let us go out like we always wanted to, I don't expect we'd of done it, 'cause we was too scared. Lawdy, chile, them was tryin' days. I sure is glad God let me live to see these days.

Olin Williams

*Age approximately 87
when interviewed in his
home at 120 Newton Street,
Athens, Georgia*

My NAME IS Olin Williams. I don't 'member what year I was born, but Marster say I was about fourteen when Freedom come. I don't 'member about my pappy 'cause he died out, and my mammy married again.

Us belonged to Marster John Whitlow, and his plantation was about three miles below Watkinsville, where Bishop is now. But there weren't nothing there then.

All the chillun my mammy had was me and my twin brother. My brother worked in the field, but I was the houseboy and helped my mammy and Mist'ess in the house, cleaned yards, and did a sight of churnin', 'cause Master sure had a lot of cows.

My job every Saturday was to scrub the wooden water buckets 'til them brass hoops shine like gold. Mist'ess would look to see if they was right, and if she find just one little spot it was all to do over.

I had to come to Watkinsville three times a week to get the mail. Mail didn't go so fast then as it do now.

Durin' the war, we had hard times and had to keep things hid out to keep the Yankees from getting 'em. I 'member one night I had a cold and was a-coughin' mighty bad. Us was hid out with the horses, and all of us was so afraid the Yankees would hear me cough and find the horses, so I got sent back to the house. We had to bury all the silver and things so as them Yankees couldn't find 'em. They didn't leave nothing they could tote.

Us had to make everything us had. Us couldn't buy nothing. There weren't no gins on our place then, so us had to pick the cotton off the seeds, wash it, and carry and spin it. Then my old auntie would weave the cloth on a loom that Marster made.

Us had to parch okra and rice for coffee, and that okra sho' was a job to parch, 'cause it was so easy to burn. It was put away in tin cans, to keep it good.

There weren't no lamps then, and us had to make candles for lights, and they sho' was a heap of trouble; they would break so easy. Us put tow string in the mold and poured the hot tallow on them. When the tallow got cold and hard, they was ready to take out of the molds.

Us had big gardens and grew all the vegetables us

could use. Us had plenty of meat, beef, hogs, chickens, and turkeys. Us had all the milk and butter us could eat, but us didn't have salt all the time. Sometimes us had to get the dirt from under the smokehouse and boil it down to get salt.

The slave quarters was shacks built out of logs, and the chimneys made of red clay and sticks, and they was all the time catchin' fire. Our shacks was in long rows with garden space 'twixt 'em, and every family had their own garden just like Marster had.

They cooked some in ovens, and there was hefty iron rods 'cross a big fireplace in the kitchen, what they swung pots on to boil things. Taters was roasted in the ashes, and they sho' was good. Us had buckets made like tubs, with handles on the sides, to carry water in, and us drunk out of gourds. There weren't no tin dippers and wash pans then. Us planted plenty gourd seed every year, and some of them gourds was great big ones.

The white folks had corded beds, and us had a big iron hook, sort of like a shoe buttoner, what us had to use to tighten up the cords in the beds 'bout twice a week. Most of the slaves had beds made of planks nailed to the side of the log shacks. They used straw ticks and sometimes feather ticks.

Marster didn't have so many slaves, and they was 'most all kinfolk. Marster had leather shoes made for us, but they looked red 'cause the leather weren't tanned.

Some white folks had overseers what was awful mean, but Marster's overseer was good to us. We didn't get whippin's, and none of us ever wanted to run away. Sometimes slaves run away from the other places and would hide out in woods and caves to keep the overseers from catchin' 'em, 'cause that meant a whippin'. Us had to have a pass to leave the place on Sunday, so the patterollers wouldn't get us.

When Freedom came, I stayed with Marster. Most all the slaves stayed on, and he fed us all just like he always done, and paid us wages besides. He was good to us all the time and took special care of any that got sick. My step-pa, Ben Moore, took my mammy and left after Freedom came and went to stay nigh High Shoals. Them Yankees marched that way, and they done took my step-pa, and us never did hear no more about him.

Us had big possum and coon hunts. Then us would have big possum suppers. Possums sure was good, baked with plenty of taters and butter, salt, and red pepper in them big old ovens. Them was good old days.

Us went to the white folks' church in Watkinsville, where Mr. Webb Langford was the preacher, and he sure was a good one. Preacher Langford baptized the niggers just like he did the white folks. They had big times, too. Big crowds would be there. Some of 'em would get so happy they would shout 'til they fell in the crick. They sung all the old-time songs: "I'm Goin' Home to Die No Mo'," "Salvation Is Free for All," and "On Jordan's Stormy Banks I Stand." It made you feel better to go to baptizin's and big meetin's. Slaves sat up in the gallery, and us had better be still and listen, elsewise old Marster sure would lay us out. White folks spent the day at church them days, and us niggers sure did like that, for they had big dinners—everything you could want, and plenty of it for all. In summertime, us carried watermelons, peaches, and all sorts of extra things to eat and stayed 'til time to get home and do the night work.

I was about eighteen when I married Laura Robinson. Laura belonged to Marster Robinson at Watkinsville. His family had done raised her, and they sure did give us a big wedding. Us married in the yard, and Preacher Langford stood on the porch; the crowd was all at the back of us. Marster and Mist'ess Robinson had invited the white folks and the slaves from all round, and us had a big supper and waiters to wait on us. We married in the evenin', just befo' night, and after supper two of our waiters got married, and us sure did have a big time, with plenty to eat and drink and dancin' all night. Me and Laura raised fourteen chillun, but the other couple never had no chillun, and they both done been dead a long time.

I 'member the first time the Klux Klan ever come round us. Us had just one child then, and us had done gone to bed. The fire was still a-burnin'; I had put on a big knot so it would be light in the room. And the door opened, and them Kluxers walked in and told me to get up and go to my marster. I sure was scared and didn't lose no time gettin' to Marster. He didn't know nothing 'bout it, and they never come no more. All the niggers sure was 'fraid of them, and that's why lots of them left the country and went to town to stay.

Cicely Cawthon
*Age 78 when interviewed
in Toccoa, Georgia*

I THINK I WAS, as well as I can remember, about five or six, maybe not that old, but I can remember nearly everything that went on 'bout the last of the war. I call myself about seventy-eight now. Course, the white folks had us down, all of us in the Bible [recorded slaves' birth dates in the family Bible]. You know how it was. You see, we couldn't any of us read.

I was one of Marster's born slaves, but my father come from Charleston, South Carolina. He was sold to my marster. He paid a thousand dollars for him and his mother—five hundred apiece for 'em. My daddy come out of the drove. His name was Charlie, Charlie Hames, and he was what you call the butler now, you know. He 'tended round the house. He never did go to the field. He drove the carriage, too. My mother's name was Harriet. She was a house girl. She had nine boys and two girls. My mother was raised there on the plantation. Marster's father raised my mother. She was one of his born slaves. My mother's mother was the cook; Icie was her name. Marster had three chillun. There was Miss Lula and Mr. Henry and the other; it died, just two living, that come to be grown.

Only thing I can remember when the Yankees come and told us we were free: Yankees had on blue coats and brass buttons. Them buttons shined like a gold dollar, all up and down, and we said, "How pretty them buttons are!" We had a big smokehouse as big as my house, and hams just piled up. The Yankees took all that from my mist'ess. They took our carriage away, too.

Marster had one of them old-time big houses. Oh Lord! It was pretty and white—so white. Everything about it was white. You don't see none like that around here now; they don't build 'em like that. Big two-story house, and two great big hickory trees hung right out over the kitchen. It was pretty, too. The dairy was under one of the hickory trees and the kitchen under the other. That was a shade for the kitchen, where us chillun could get out and play.

Everything inside of Marster's house was mahogany. Them had curtains round the beds—tall beds with them high posts. That's all the kind of beds they had, except little trundle beds you could slip under the big bed in the daytime; night, pull it out and put the chillun to sleep. All the dishes was flowered. I don't know as I ever saw a plain plate except in the quarters. They had blue-and-yellow flowered plates, cups and saucers flowered, too, and great, big, long, covered dishes to match. There was great big goblets they used for every day; they held about three cups, not like the ones they use now, shaped different. Mist'ess had a set of fine glass she hardly ever used 'cept for mighty special company; mighty special company had to come 'fore you could go in the sideboard and get 'em, 'cause they was easy broke. That big sideboard, um! Mahogany, the finest thing! I ain't seen one like that! Well, I did, too. I saw one time since, like it, in Atlanta.

Our kitchen was off from the big house. The kitchen was bigger than this house. And that fireplace! I never saw such a big one. The sticks of wood for the fireplace was twelve feet long. There was hooks—two big hooks up in the chimney. I've seen 'em hang lambs' and calves' hindquarters up in that chimney to smoke. You know, they'd kill more than they could eat and didn't have ice like they do now to keep things from spoiling, so they hung 'em up in the chimney to smoke. How good! The sweetest stuff you ever ate in your life!

I'm going to tell you, I know Marster had close on to a hundred slaves. Oh! He had darkies there I didn't know nothing 'bout. Cabins? Must have been 'bout fifty cabins in the quarters. Darkies slept on straw mattresses, all of 'em. Course, they had plenty of quilts and cover. When they threshed every year, they throwed that old straw out and put new straw in. They didn't have no chinches like they do now. Them log cabins was clean; they didn't have no chinches. The logs was fixed with mud. Mud was made up after the cabin was built and packed in the chinks, and when they got hard no wind couldn't get you. Sticks and mud was used to build the chimneys, too.

They allowanced slaves their rations once a week. It was something to see all the vittles that come from the smokehouse once a week—syrup, meal, flour, bacon, a big hunk if there was a family. Slaves didn't have cows, but there was plenty of cows on the place. Every darky would bring his cup to the dairy and get milk; great big things like measuring cups, they'd hold from a quart to a half-gallon, different from the cups they got now. Slaves could get vegetables. Every colored family had a little place near their cabin to raise vegetables on if they wanted to. They didn't get no coffee; they drank milk. Nobody 'cept the old women drank coffee.

They had a passel of old women, about a dozen or two of 'em, that stayed in the house and minded the chillun while the others went to the fields. They had cradles they laid 'em in, and little ticks for the cradles. Them ticks was made and dyed at home. Some of 'em was blue and some what you might call clay color. That was all them old women had to do, and they had better take good care of them babies. They was careful—just as careful of you as a breed sow if you was going to have chillun. But they'd sell you off if you didn't have any.

Darky women wore white-and-blue striped dresses, spun and wove. Them that lived in the quarters had looms and reels. They spun their own cloth and made their own clothes. They made everything they wore 'cept shoes. Uncle Jeff Hames, the shoemaker, he made the shoes that all of 'em wore on the place. He was about the first slave Marster had. He come from Virginny. They paid big money for him 'cause he was a valuable darky. He was 'bout as valuable as the blacksmith. I don't remember how much they paid for him, but it was big money.

Marster had sheep. In cold weather, women wore woolen dresses and coats—they called 'em jackets—and woolen stockings, and the men wore woolen socks and britches, too. Everything they had was woven and made on the place. You didn't see any of 'em with a hat on those days. Our white folks didn't buy no hats for us. When we went to preaching, we had to go clean. I had a white pique bonnet with buttons. I thought bonnets looked mighty pretty when they done 'em up with flour starch. People don't make flour starch now. People don't know how to make flour starch now.

My wedding dress was made of white lawn with tucks and frills—long, pretty, too. One of Mist'ess's nieces let me have her wedding veil, and I wore it. Fine, too! A colored man named John Glauster married us. You know, he was just a man on the place what sung and prayed, and he could give out the hymns. He was the preacher, Glauster was, for marryin' and buryin' folks.

We belonged to the white folks' church, but we didn't go in at the door of the church, though. They had a stairway on the outside where we could go up, and then after we got up the stairs we'd be in church, in the gallery.

Mist'ess had a book. It was a catechism, and she asked us all the questions every Sunday. Marster let us have preachin' in our cabins, too. Mist'ess had a book on a table in her room. I saw it. I saw pictures in it, and I asked her what it was, and she read it to me just like a child. She read it to me, she told me the story, and she lectured to me. Mist'ess's favorite songs was "Come Ye That Love the Lord" and "I'm Bound for the Promised Land" and "On Jordan's Stormy Banks I Stand." Mist'ess liked 'em, and I liked 'em, too. "Hark from the Tomb" and "Come, solemn sisters,/Weep around, and drop a tear./We've lost a sister from our side,/She's gone beyond the skies" was songs we used at funerals.

Poor white folks used to hang around the quarters, and if they could beat you out of anything, they did. They'd trade the slaves out of their rations for calico and stuff. Some of the darkies sold their meat and meal, but if it was found out they got a good whipping.

The overseer on the plantation had a horn, a great big ram's horn. I never did see such a big horn. It was 'bout two feet long. The overseer blowed it about two hours before day. The darkies had to get up and cook their breakfast and curry their mules and start for the field. They had better be in that field by sunup. When the sun went down, they stuck their hoes up in the field and quit. Then they was free for the day.

I've seen slaves sold. I just can remember 'em up on the block with white men making bids. They was a lot of white men there, and they bid them off, and the highest bidder got 'em, just like they do at auctions.

Darkies had particular tasks to perform. Now, like if they was gathering up corn, they shucked corn late to get it in the crib to keep it from being rained on. Sometimes, if they didn't get through before dark, they held torches to see by.

Overseers didn't do no more than what Marster told him to. He'd come to the field, and if he saw a slave sitting under a tree he'd ask him if he was sick, and it was all right if he was sick, but if he was well and laying out under a tree he got a whipping. The overseer would go back and tell Marster, and that night he'd give 'em just as many licks as Marster said. But he was careful with the darkies. I never saw the overseer with a billy in his hand. His whip was wrapped around the horn of his saddle. He'd unwrap it and give you whatever Marster said. Overseers didn't have no rules, but if you resisted him he'd double your whipping. For killing time or being lazy, you got twenty-five licks; for stealing, fifty licks; and for running away—that was the worst—if they got you back, you got a hundred licks.

I had a cousin to run away, and they got her back from Charleston. The overseer give her a hundred licks. One lick cut the blood, and my mist'ess got so mad she throwed that long hair back—I can see that long hair now—and quarreled at Marster. He said he had to make a example for the other slaves. Mist'ess said it injured the woman to whip her that way, so then Marster made 'em be more careful. Even that weren't as bad as going to the chain gang now. Young darkies gets mad with me for saying that, but they protected you, and nobody didn't need to bother you. They protected you wherever you went.

We had one man to run away to the North. He run away because the overseer whipped him because he went to the adjoining plantation to see a woman. You had to have a' pass to go off the place, and he went without a pass. They never did hear nothing of him. They put the hounds on his trail, but they never did catch him. Mist'ess said there was a trick in it somewhere.

My mother was Marster's house girl. People didn't do like they do now. She'd be called a chambermaid now. I just stayed around the house with Mist'ess. I was just, you might say, her little keeper. I stayed around and waited on her, handed her water, fanned her, kept the flies off her, pulled up her pillow, and done anything she'd tell me to do. My mother combed her hair and dressed her, too. Her hair was long. She could sit on it. It was a light color, and it was so pretty! I'd call it silver.

Our marster kept patterollers to keep us straight. There was some hardheaded darkies like they is now who wanted to go without a pass, and if they didn't have a pass the patterollers got 'em and brought 'em back home. There's a song about the patterollers:

"Run, nigger, run, the patteroll will catch you,
Run, nigger, run, the patteroll will catch you,
Run, nigger, run, the patteroll will catch you,
You better get away, you better get away."

Yes'm, they had Ku Klux all through the country, but they never whipped my daddy. After some of the darkies was free, they got bigoty and wanted to act so. The white folks put things over their faces and come around and scared us to death, but they never did do nothing to any of our niggers. I was 'fraid they would. Mist'ess was 'fraid they might do something to my daddy 'cause he [was] one of the uppity ones, so she had him to stay home at night, and they didn't get him. He was the carriage driver, and she was 'fraid for him.

We used to play lots of games, such as Turning the Tin Pan and Who's Got the Thimble? The one with the thimble in his hand last had to pay a pawn. Grown-up darkies made one another kiss or pay a forfeit. Another game we played was Walking to Jerusalem. They'd blindfold you and spin you around. If you missed the gate, you had a pawn to pay.

In them days, darkies wore beads. Babies wore beads around their necks. You wouldn't see a baby without beads. They was made of glass and looked like diamonds. They had 'em in different colors, too—white, blue, and red, little plaited strings of beads. When their necks got bigger, they wore another kind, on 'til they got grown. They trimmed hats with beads, ladies and chillun, too. Mist'ess had a hat that cost fifty thousand dollars, just covered with beads, light blue all over, and turned right up in front. It had a bow of ribbon, a big bow tied by her right ear. All that long hair like silver and that little beaded bonnet sitting up on her head sho' was pretty. That great big bulk of hair looked like a curled snake back there. My!

Marster wore a black beaver hat. How it shined! He wore high collars and little bow ties. His cuffs was long, with two buttons on 'em. He wore broadcloth—black broadcloth—all the time on Sunday. He had white linen shirts, too. There was four studs in his shirt bosom, and he had high boots.

Marster had a tin box. He kept it in the closet when it wasn't so heavy, but he kept it under his bed at night after cotton-picking time. He had two bulldogs, the meanest-looking dogs. They'd look at you and roll their eyes. I was 'fraid of them dogs. Course, when I got to the house every morning, my daddy had the dogs blocked. He'd have 'em chained. Them was the meanest-looking dogs! I never see any bulldogs now that look like that.

Marster had two stables of horses. The carriage horses and the other horses—two stables. And Lawd, I can't tell you the number of mules. They were too many for me to tell you—'bout four or five hundred, I reckon. And eggs! Me and my auntie have brought Miss Sue 'bout two bushels of eggs a day. Sometimes hens set way off in the woods, and we never knowed nothing 'bout it 'til they come up with a big gang of chickens. Marster had a big place, but I don't know how many acres. I've heard him say he had never set foot on some of the land his father give him.

They was haints in them days. Mist'ess said a man died and buried a pot of money, and he wanted his son to have the money, and his son didn't get it, so he come back and set it on the chimney. He was naked—think of that, a naked man! And he asked Marster to get up and follow him, took him out behind the chimney, showed him a place, and told him to dig. Marster dug all night, and 'fore the sun come up the haint wanted to get away, so Marster got another man to help him, and they found a big pot of money. It took 'em both to lift up the pot—a big iron wash pot, bigger than the big wash pot Mist'ess had at the spring. The haint told him to send for his son and give it to him, so Marster done it, and the haint never come back. Mist'ess told me about it.

It was real funny to hear the darkies call their stock. They'd say, "Soo-oo-oo-k, Spot! Whoo-oo-ie. Whoo-oo-ie! Come on to your breakfast! Come on to your supper!" And every man's hog would go to its place, and cows, too. When Uncle Ponder stood there and called at the drawbars—they didn't have no fences then—they'd all come running, and every one knowed where its stall was. Sometimes four or five men would milk.

When darkies got sick, they had herbs in the house. Senna was what they give you if you was bilious. It growed in the garden. Mist'ess had a bed of it. That's what she give you instead of salts. To keep off typhoid fever, if you could smell fever on you, she'd make a cup of purge grass, and that fever would break up. St. John leaves was good for chills and fever. White plantain tea was for weakly women. 'Bout the only things slave needed to keep off diseases was good stout shoes on their feet, plenty to eat, good clothes, and when it started raining to quit work and come in. They had shelters in the fields for the men to go to if it started raining.

We had lots of fun on holidays. On New Year's Day, we didn't work, but we didn't have this Fourth of July and all this mess—Labor Day and this carrying-on. Then Christmas Day was something else! If I could call back one of them Christmas Days now, when I went up to the house and brung back my checkered wagon full! Lord, I was so happy! Great big round peppermint balls! They have peppermint sticks now, but it wasn't so then. Big bunches of raisins. We put apronsful on the bed and went back to the house to get another apronful.

We had good times at corn shuckings, too. Honey, I've seen my grandma Icie, the cook, when they had corn shuckings, the chickens she'd put in that pot! The big pot hanging on one of them hooks in the kitchen fireplace—I ain't ever seen a pot that big since. I don't see 'em in the stores now. They don't have 'em. She put twelve chickens in that pot, grown hens, let 'em boil, put the dumplings in, called the darkies, and give 'em a plateful. Lawdy, honey, I just wish you coulda been there and seen how my grandma made that gingerbread—what you called raised gingerbread. They cooked that for corn shuckings and used it for cake. It was better than what cake is now. And they give 'em locust beer to drink with it, not this stuff they sell in bottles now, they call beer.

We had dances after the corn shuckings. After they got through, the fiddler would start to fiddling, and they would ring up in an old-time square dance. Everybody danced off to themselves. Just let your foot go backward and then let your foot go forward and whirl around. Men, too, danced that way, by themselves, and you could hear them darkies laugh! Weren't nothing in 'em, no whiskey. My! They had a good time! Wasn't no killing in them days, no liquor, no cussing, no saying "lying fool" to one another like 'tis now, no rough doings. There wasn't a pistol on that place but what was up at the house. There wasn't no killings then.

When we had cotton pickings, just like corn shuckings, there was good things to eat and a dance afterwards. When we got through threshing, Marster give us a picnic. Marster didn't have to go off the place for nothing. He raised flour, too. When they threshed wheat, Lawd have mercy! This lot wouldn't hold the straw. Then that was the time for our summer picnic. We'd have good things to eat, like at corn shuckings, and Marster would give every one of the men a dram. Marster drawed it himself, had a big tin cup, and he'd take half a cupful for two men. But didn't nobody get drunk nor bother nobody.

A big keg of whiskey set in the dining room. It had a bung in it—you know what I'm talking about—and nobody didn't bother it. It just set there in the dining room. That was for the medicine. Aunt Rachel would come up to the house and get a little bit to carry down to the cabin for breast milk for her baby. Huh! Doctors wouldn't like that now.

When Marster's chillun got married, we all saw the wedding. From the yard back down to what you call the first orchard, all the darkies gathered. Every darky from the quarters was there, men and women, too. After it was through, all the darkies passed by the bride and groom, and each one, men and women, said, "Oh, God bless you, Marster!" and squat. That's what we called dropping a curtsy. If the wedding was at a church, all the darkies come, and when the bride and groom come out and stood on the steps all the darkies passed by and dropped a curtsy. It makes 'em feel good for all the darkies to say that to 'em.

The wedding dresses had trails as far as you could see. It took two folks to hold 'em up. My mother carried young Mist'ess's trail, but course after she carried the trail in the church she went back to a place where she couldn't see, where the darkies was. Then when young Mist'ess come out of the church, she picked up the trail and carried it again. All the time, when she would get in the carriage, her maid would hold up her trail for her. Sometimes I tell that and people don't believe me.

Harriet Benton

Age 82 when interviewed
at her home in
Columbus, Georgia, in 1936

As a slave girl, I belonged to Mr. Jim O'Neal, a Troup County planter. My father, who was half Indian, one-fourth white, and one-fourth nigger, always claimed that he was born a free man. He was a native of the Tidewater region of Virginia and often spoke of the fine fish and oysters that he used to catch and enjoy when a boy. During the 1830s, when he was a young man, Yankee speculators caught my father, brought him South, and sold him into slavery. I don't know where Mr. O'Neal bought him, but I know that the master treated him very kindly and that my father always had spending money. I was never hungry or without plenty of good clothes to wear—including shoes—until after the war.

As a child, I played hide-and-seek, Stealing Bases, and other games with the white children. Of course, I looked up to my white folks but thought of us all—white and black—as belonging to the same family. The white boys and the slave boys all played and frolicked together, climbed trees, shelled black walnuts, hunted muscadines, gather chestnuts, fished, and did about everything together that younger boys ever did on a farm.

I never knew of any slaves fighting or gambling or getting drunk. And they not only loved their owners but were loyal and faithful to them throughout the Civil War period. Occasionally, a Negro was whipped for stealing—just as they ought to be whipped now for taking things that don't belong to them.

When the Yankees came through in '65, one of them, I remember, picked up my little brother and kissed him. Then they burned nearly everything on the place they couldn't carry off, and stole the balance.

I WAS BORNED the middle of a January on a Thursday, so I was told. The Bible what had the dates in it got burned up, and it was durin' slavery times. I was borned belongin' to Mr. Marse John Anderson, a big merchant in Danburg, Wilkes County, Georgia.

He, Marse John, bought my mother from his pa's estate, givin' one thousand dollars in money for her, and she not but eleven years old! He bought my father from Mrs. Anthony after she was deceased. She left it so her darkies could choose out who they wanted to buy them, and he chose Marse John 'cause he such a great man. The greatest thing of all was that he was a Baptist and had a Christian heart, and he proved it to the whole world. He was as great a man as was in all Georgia, and he was a big merchant, and it was natural he had seven hundred customers at a time and over four thousand acres of land when he died. When he finished his days on earth, he left for the Glory Land, he did. He didn't believe in ever owin' nobody nothin', and he raised me like that. Why, I been goin' all round on the streets this evenin' lookin' for Mr. R. Wynne to pay him my house rent for last month.

My pa was a fine mechanic. Him and his brother made the buggy Marse John went a-courtin' in. He use to make buggies and do all kinds of work like that for people in Danburg.

I was a little boy big enough to keep in memory my young marster gettin' ready to go to the Confederate war. Then he come back. I 'member I saw him a-comin' a long distance away, but he had on strange clothes, not his uniform. And I ran to meet him, and he said afterwards that I jumped up on him, I was so glad to see him, but I don't 'member that part of it. After he come back from the war, he called up all the darkies, and he stood on the porch and talked to 'em and said, "You-all is free, just as free as I is." But they wouldn't leave him; they all remained on 'cause he was so good to 'em.

In the year 1874, Marse John put me on a wagon to haul freight every day from Washington to Danburg—twelve miles, twenty-four miles round trip. I went every day 'scusin' Sundays. At first, I drive two mules, and then I got up to four. I had to get up way before day to make the trip on time.

Long 'bout that time, the stagecoach quit runnin' from Washington, Georgia, to Abbeville, South Carolina, and the folks in Danburg missed the mail that the stage brought 'em. So one day, Marse John and some more white gentlemen from Danburg got in their buggies and come all the way here to Washington and had me sworn in to take the mail every day. They had me prepared so I could take it for 'em. After that, I took the mail every day, and I was thus the first daily mail carrier in the county of Wilkes. I is proud that the white folks trusted me that way with their mail.

Besides all that, the men use to give me big sums of money to bring to town for 'em, mostly to buy things for 'em. I 'member once Marse John give me exactly $303 to bring to a man here, and I brought it to him that day. I handed it to him and told him Marse John Anderson sent it to him. I waited respectful like, and he counted it and said, "That's all right, Wesley. Tell John you fetched it to me." I said, "Yes, sir, but I wants a receipt." He said, "No need of one. You brought me the money." And I waited with my hat in my hand, and he fretted like, "What you waitin' for?" I said, "My receipt." With that, he tore off a piece of brown paper and wrote on it and stuck it at me and didn't say nothin'. I thanked him and went on. But I'd of waited there all night but what I'd carried back a receipt. I wasn't goin' to have Marse John havin' to pay that $303 again on my account. You see, I knowed that man, and Marse John did, too.

Marse John asked him next time he saw him what made him write on brown paper. He laughed and said, "Well, that boy you sent here with that money has got sense."

Enough times, I have come to this town with over five hundred dollars in my vest pocket pinned up in a envelope. I would count out what it would take to buy what was wanted at one place and go in and buy that, and then go way off out of sight where nobody could see me and take out enough money to pay for what I had to get at another place and buy that. No, sir, I never did let nobody see me handle all the money I had on me! Even in them times, somebody might have knocked me out and took the white folks' money 'way from me. I use to bring cotton, too, and sell it for the men.

Sixty-three years ago come this Christmas, I married Peggy Booker. Us married the Christmas of the year 1877 and been livin' together ever since. I married Peggy, and then I quit courtin'. Marse John let us have his nice buggy, and we drove over to Marse Preacher Fortson's—he was a brother-in-law of Marse John's—and he married us standin' up in the hall of his big house. I could have married lots more gals if I had wanted to, 'cause I was black and nice lookin' and have been well brought up and knew how to work and make a honest livin', but I loved Peggy, and I have taken good care of her since. We had fifteen children born to us but didn't raise but eleven of 'em. Peggy is paralyzed now and can't do nothin' to help herself, but she been good to me and took care of me and the children. Now

I take care of her. I 'members the vows what I took there 'fore Preacher Fortson when he married us, and I 'tends to do all I can for her as long as she lives. I go to the druggists here and buys physic for her, and they all knows me, and if I don't have the money it is just the same; I can get what I need, 'cause they knows I'm goin' to pay 'em when I get it.

I hauled freight and carried mail to Danburg, Wilkes County, Georgia, for ten years and would have continued on, but Peggy wanted me to give it up. She worried over it so, me havin' to make that long trip every day and in all kinds of weather, so to oblige her 'cause she loved me and wanted to take good care of me, I give it up. But I couldn't tell Marse John I wouldn't haul for him no more, so to get out of it I told him I'd continue on if he would pay me three hundred dollars a year and furnish me a whole lot of rations every week. I knowed all the time it was too much and that he weren't going to do it, but that was my way of getting round hurtin' his feelin's by quittin'.

I come off the wagon and went to farmin'. I'm a good farmer; I always could make money out of the ground. I lived round first with Marse John and then with Mr. Walter Sutton, there in Danburg. I kind of divided my time 'twixt 'em like.

I reckon 'long 'bout here is where my religious experience come in. On a Wednesday when the earthquake was, 'bout 1886, I was shook up and stirred up in my heart more greater than anything 'fore that, and I raised up in bed that night while the earth was a-shakin', and

I promised the Lord secretly if he would jest not kill me, then I'd serve Him long as I lived. I made a contract with Him that night.

I went and joined the church that year the earthquake was, and I felt called to preach, and I prayed secretly to get rid of it, but God had work for me to do like when he called Moses, and I took the job. So I prayed on, and the more I prayed the more the call come down on me, the more I was 'prest [sure] that I had to preach, 'til on a second Sunday, when Peggy had dressed up and gone to her church, and the children had gone over to they grandma's, and I was at home by myself. I took up the Bible—it was my steppa's Bible—and I opened it like this to the first Gospel of Matthew at the second chapter.

And that was my evidence, 'cause I had not been to school nor college. All the schoolin' I had was in the year 1873. I went on Sundays that year to learn to read and took my old Webster's blue-back spellin' book, and all the farther I got in that was *baker*, and about all I learned was my letters and figures. So when I, the first time I looked inside of a Bible, found I could read, I knowed I was spiritually called. But I kept prayin' and reading secretly. Still, I didn't know about trying preachin'. And I tried other things, playin' round like Jonah did, and like him I didn't get nowhere—lost 'most everything I had. So finally, I gave up and went before the church and asked to be examined to preach.

They wouldn't try me, and for fifteen long years I was laid on the table of that church. They wouldn't admit me 'cause I had never been educated, they said. They said they wanted finished men—one what went to college, one what knowed how to preach. I come like the inchworm, little by little 'til I got there, and they wanted men what come the grasshopper way, all in one jump. I didn't have no college wings. That is when preachers get up and use big words what go flyin' over folks' heads, and debates the Bible, and goes on [about] all such foolishness as what half what hears 'em don't know what he's talking 'bout. They like that 'cause it sounds big, but there ain't nothin' to it—nothin' but sound, that's all.

I kept a-waitin', so they sent for me at a conference. They took me off down to the schoolhouse, two preachers and a whole passel of deacons did, to examine me to find out if I knew anything. They didn't think I'd make the grade, so they took me off to myself. The first question they asked me was "What is preachin'?" I answered, "Preachin' is the power of God unto salvation unto all that believeth." I made the grade by answerin' the first question they asked me. They was astonished then and stopped right there. They put a Bible and a hymn book in my hand and said, "As you have received these, go preach and teach."

I didn't say nothin', but I sought wisdom by prayer and readin' my Bible, and now I been a member of the Baptist Church over fifty years and a preacher a long time, and I been recognized and appreciated as a man of God all that time. The earthquake did shake me up and start me off right. I preach now when they call on me. But I ain't one of these newfangled preachers what uses big words and has a college education—college wings, I call it. They think if you been to college you got everything—can just spread your arms and fly on. But I'm here to tell 'em they can't. That ain't the way; you got to pray for the wisdom and the power. They all crank up and go ridin' off to Sunday school and church now and don't pay no 'tention to them what can't go. Why, I had to lecture some of the preachers and members 'bout neglectin' Peggy, I did. Now they come to see her and bring her the Lord's Supper, 'count of her can't go to church on Communion days like she use to. I told 'em good 'bout it and stirred 'em up. I tells 'em when they don't do their duty. I'm a preacher, too, and so I can talk plain to 'em.

Oh, yes, there is one thing I want to tell you 'bout, something most folks don't know happened. I recollect it good. And that was, just after the Confederate war there came a lot of men and camped there below Danburg, and they done lots of mischief, stealin' all the horses they could lay hands on. Why, the folks that heard they was there took all they horses down and hid them out in the Broad River swamps—'bout thirty-five or forty fine horses was hid out all 'long down the river. These folks took a rail fence down that was round a pasture and moved it right smack 'cross the big public road. They done all kinds of bad things like that to pester the good people of Danburg, Wilkes County, Georgia.

Danburg folks wouldn't have nothin' to do with 'em. No, sir, they wouldn't. They was above such as that. But one day, they come ridin' up with great pistols on their saddles, and they had fine saddles, too, and they had horses shod but wouldn't pay for it. Marse John Anderson and some more gentlemen was at the blacksmith shop, and Marse John was fixed for 'em, 'cause he wasn't scared of 'em. So he went and shook his finger at 'em—nothin' but his finger—and said, "You-all is goin' round doin' all the mischief you can, prowlin' and stealin' and everything like that. You is mean and low-down, and you ain't nothin' but Wheeler's old cavalry, that's all you is, just his mean old cavalry, I know." He quarreled with 'em, and they didn't say nothin' back to him. They took what he said and just laughed, 'cause they saw he wasn't scared of 'em. So one day right after that, they picked up and left, and as they passed through they was singin' loud as they could,

"Here's Wheeler's cavalry.
Wheeler's in the field.
If he gets wounded,
It'll be by a wagon wheel."

Lots of darkies went off with 'em, and they went a-whoopin' and a-hollerin' and a-singin' that song. I 'member that, and how glad everybody was that they had gone.

I'm doin' regular farm work now but ain't farmin' for myself. The good white man what I worked with last wouldn't rent me no land, said I was too old to plow. That sho' did hurt my feelin's. I'm old, I know—well up in the eighties—but I'm goin' to work just as long as I can. I walk three miles to my work every mornin'. I get up, eat my breakfast, and reach up, and there is my dinner bucket the children have fixed for me the night before, and I take my stick and off I go and am at work 'fore the hands on the farm I help on is there. I can do more hard work now than these ordinary Negroes what has come on since slavery. They're not taught to work. They're not bred and born good as us what come 'long way back yonder, when folks knew how to work and how to take care of theirselves.

The government started givin' me a old-age pension—five dollars a month—but twelve months ago come this January they cut me off and said I would have to wait awhile and let some of the other old folks have some help, too. I need it mighty bad, 'specially since Peggy is sick, but I go on and do the best I can and trusts the Lord. I'm goin' to work as long as I live. I got three homes I can go to any day—three good white men what know me and want me to come live with 'em. But I rent a little house down here on the Augusta Highway four miles from town, and I stay there and pay my rent every month. It makes me independent, to live like that and work for my livin'. It is more 'spectable.

Martha Everette

*Age 85 when interviewed
at her son's home in
Hawkinsville, Georgia*

I WAS BORN IN PULASKI COUNTY. 'Bout twelve miles from Hawkinsville. Maw had five chillun, and I was next to the oldest. But the oldest one died, so that just left me and the three others.

Our marster was old Mr. Jim Lathrop, and he sho' was rich. He was born up North, but course he come down South befo' I was born, I reckon. He owned 'bout a thousand acres of land and two hundred niggers. Mr. Lathrop didn't live on the plantation, though; he lived in Savannah. But he and his wife and three chillun would come to the plantation a heap of times and stay weeks at the time. He had white overseers to tend to the place.

I 'members four of 'em, and there may have been more. Anyhow, when Marster'd come, he'd stay with one of them overseers. The house was a big log house, and it had five rooms and a hall and a porch.

Marster owned a lot of stock. He had three milkers, and sometimes they'd milk seventy-five to eighty-five head of cows at one time. And we raised most everything on that farm—cotton, corn, taters, anything anybody else down here growed. The crops was carried to Hawkinsville to market. We did some of our tradin' there, but sometimes Marster sent us things from Savannah.

My daddy worked in the field, and so did Maw sometimes. She'd cook for the white folks a week, and then another woman would cook and Maw would work in the field. My brothers and sisters was too little to work. The first work I ever 'member doin' was totin' water to the field hands when I was 'bout ten. Then me and two other little gals had to wait on the table. We had to clean up the house, too. Them floors was kept shinin'.

Didn't nobody whip me 'cept my maw, and she meant business! Chillun couldn't do then like they can now. Maw'd be settin' in a room, and us chillun'd come in. She'd look at us, and all she'd have to do was scrape her foot and we'd fly under the house. We knew better than not to mind. We'd go under the house and eavesdrop, but she never knew it. Marster never did whip none of his niggers, but the overseer'd whip the grown ones if they didn't do right. We was all treated well.

The grown niggers had dances on Saturday nights, but they wouldn't let us chillun go. We'd peep and see all we could, though. On the Fourth of July, we always had a big dinner, and it was all spread on a long table. Whoever raised the first tater would put it in the middle of the table so everybody could see it. We'd 'most always have a big fish fry, and along with the fish we'd have barbecue, chicken, cakes, pies, and everything else that was good. Marster would come from Savannah then, and he and the overseers would invite some of their white friends. At Christmastime, the overseers let us have candy pullin's and tell us that was our Santy Claus.

We sho' did go to church. We'd pile in two horse wagons and go to the Baptist church at Blue Spring. The white folks sat in front, and we sat in the back. When the preacher got through preachin' to the white folks, they'd leave, and then he'd preach to us. We had prayer meetin's every Wednesday night in the different nigger cabins.

Every Sunday mornin', the rations was give out. And there'd be plenty, too. It wasn't just a little bit like folks give now. It was enough to last a week. Every day, we'd have greens, meat, taters, flour and cornbread, syrup, and all the milk and butter we could use. On Sundays, we'd have chicken and cake. We could eat in them days, but we can't eat much now. We raised our own wheat, so we had flour all the time. Everything we ate was raised on the plantation 'cept sugar and coffee.

Lots of times, the slaves would go fishin' in a pond

right there on the place. I 'member one time the grown folks decided to take us chillun with them, so they had us all in a wagon and told us we better not get out. We set there while they was fishin', and pretty soon I saw somethin' wigglin' in the grass. I forgot all 'bout what they told me not to do and hopped right out of the wagon and picked up the thing I thought was a fish. It wasn't no fish at all, but a long snake. Maw wore me out then and there for not mindin' her.

The overseers' wives learned some of the nigger women to sew, so they made most of 'em [the clothes]. Some of the cloth was spun and woven right there on the place. Sometimes Marster'd send us clothes from Savannah.

Whenever I hear a screech owl, I know somebody's gonna die. I heard a preacher say once that if you hear a cow bellowin', you could look out for death in a week or two. If a dog howls at night, that's a sho' sign of death. But I don't believe nothin' 'bout that sneezin'-while-eatin' business; sometimes you just gets choked, and that's why you sneeze. I always stop the clock and hang a cloth over the mirror if somebody dies in the house.

I 'member one day, one of the white neighbors told one of our overseers that the Yankees was comin', but he just said, "Well, let 'em come." I was right by the door, and pretty soon I looked up, and I saw the biggest crowd of white people comin'. Them was the Yankees, and me and all the other chillun was scared to death. They stopped at the gates, and the leader wouldn't let 'em go in, but he went to the door and asked the overseer for somethin' to eat. That overseer use to live in the North, so he told him to walk in and help hisself. All the other soldiers went to the back door and was fed from there. Some of 'em come two or three times after that, but they never did bother nobody; they just come for somethin' to eat.

I 'member when they captured Jeff Davis. All us chillun was in the yard, and we heard the drums just a-beatin'. We ran in the house and told Miss Car'line—she was an overseer's wife—'bout it, but she told us we'd better not leave the yard. She said it was 'bout eight or nine miles off, and we wanted to go, but she wouldn't let us. Course, we didn't know what had happened then, but later we heard that they'd got Jeff Davis.

When the war was over, the overseers told us we was free and could go where we pleased; but we all stayed right there 'til Christmas. Maw's brother was workin' on a farm near Abbeville, and he wanted her to work down there with him. She decided to go at Christmastime, so she took all the chillun with her. My daddy stayed on at the plantation, but he'd come to see us. I never did see no mo' of my marster after we moved. The next thing I heard was that he and his wife was dead.

Randall Flagg

Age 86 when interviewed
at his home in
Columbus, Georgia

MY FORMER OWNER was Colonel Tom Ragland, of Alabama. When the old Eagle Cotton Mill was built on the present site of the Eagle and Phoenix Mills, my master loaned or hired me to the contractors, for whom I worked as a water boy on that job. Colonel Mott owned and operated a gristmill where the old Eagle Cotton Mill was built. This gristmill, I remember, had to be torn down to make room for the cotton mill.

Later, in '65, when the soldiers of General Wilson burned the Eagle Mill, I was in Columbus, and I saw the whole town in a blaze, a sight that made a very deep and lasting impression upon me.

I knowed nothing of my parents' antecedents; they were simply slaves, though I think my mother was born near Milledgeville, Georgia, and my master did not own my father.

When a small boy, I used to lie under the looms and tie threads for Aunt Mary, one of Mr. Ragland's expert loom hands.

There were patterollers in those days, but I never saw or heard of a slave being whipped in my life. We slaves were well fed, well clothed, and given proper medical attention when ill. We weren't fed fancy foods, but we were furnished good, substantial, wholesome foods, such as meat, meal, rice, coffee, flour, sugar, molasses, peas, potatoes, and vegetables. During the summer months, we also had berries, fruits, and melons, and at hog-killing time were given fresh meat. We were provided with good shoes, warm clothes in winter, and light, cool clothes in summer.

The white and colored children, up to eight or ten years of age, played and frolicked together. Sometimes the little darkies would dispute among themselves as to which of his master's little sons they belonged. One little Negro would say, "I belongs to so-and-so." "No, you don't. I am his nigger. You belongs to so-and-so," another would say.

Of course, we slave boys were made to do certain chores by the time we were large enough. The first work that I ever did was feeding my master's hogs. And when he loaned me to the contractors as a water boy on the old Eagle construction job, I felt very proud and important. Oftentimes one of the bosses would say, "Son, aren't you tired, don't you want to lie down and rest—sleep—awhile?" And I would say, "No, sir." And about that time, someone on the job would yell, "Water boy!"—just what I had been waiting to hear—and off I would go on the run with my jug and gourd. We didn't have tin and coconut-shell drinking cups and dippers in those days.

My mother deserted my daddy and went away with the Yankees in 1865 and didn't return until 1870. When she came back, I was working on the Russell County, Alabama, plantation of Judge Jim Johnson [at one time a governor of Georgia], father of the late Honorable Walter Johnson of Columbus. The overseer on the Johnson plantation paid me two dollars a month, with some food and clothes thrown in, to mind the judge's cattle. That was all I did—just mind cattle.

Later, I moved to Judge Johnson's Chattahoochee County, Georgia, plantation, and there I was with the judge and attended him during his last illness. When he died, I assisted Mr. Buriel Williams in preparing his body for burial. Then I hauled his corpse in a two-horse wagon to Cusseta and shipped it by rail to Columbus, coming with it and attending his burial in Linwood Cemetery.

Alonzo "Lonnie" Pondley
*Age 80 when interviewed
in his home in Athens, Georgia*

WELL, I WAS BORN in Madison County, six miles from Danielsville, about eighty years ago, in 1859. I was a slave, but a happy one. My young mist'ess and marster's names were Nancy and John Lester. My father's marster's name was Jimmie Nunn. He lived on the Danielsville Road. My father would have to get a pass from Mr. Jimmie to come to see my mother. You see, they were on different plantations. He got to come to see my mother twice a week. If he slipped out without the pass, the patterollers got after him, and if he outran them and got back to his marster he was safe, but if he didn't he got a whipping. Twenty-five licks was what he would get.

As far back as I can remember is when us little niggers was just big enough to run around. Mist'ess would be so good to us. She would always pay us in some way to help her. She would say, "Bring me some water. Get me some on the north side of the spring, so it will be cool." Or "Pick up some bark for me, and I will make some candy for my little niggers." Lawd, you ought to have seen us little niggers scramble after that water and pick up those chips. My mist'ess would not let anyone whip us, not even my mother or father.

Oh, we were the happiest little souls in the world. Old Miss would never consult a doctor. She was as good as any of them. When we got sick, we would holler, "Old Mist'ess!" and she would come a-running and ask, "What is the matter with my little niggers now?" "My belly hurts," I'd say. She always kept some medicine made of chinaberry roots. "Now take this, and Mist'ess will give you some candy."

My grandma was the cook. She would throw on a ten-foot pole and let it burn to ashes and then make pones of bread. She would then put them in the ashes, and when they cooked awhile she took the shovel and throw ashes over them. When they were done, she took them out, washed them, and greased them. They was good. We would go to the bottoms and find mussel shells; that is where we got our spoons that we ate with. We had plenty to eat. You see, Mist'ess and young Marster wanted their niggers to grow up healthy like our father. He was a big, healthy nigger. They would say, "It ain't no trouble for a big, healthy nigger to get married."

I remember one time they was sending us out to hoe cotton. I decided I didn't want to go, so I pitched a big fit. Instead of hoeing the cotton, I laid down and started grabbing it with my teeth. Marster came out and sent me to the house. He said I never would amount to nothing. He didn't let me go to the field no more that year. He thought I was sick.

There was plenty of potatoes, corn, wheat, and everything else that is raised on a farm, but Marster would never raise over one bale of cotton. We had oxcarts in those days. I can remember when it took two weeks to go to Augusta and back with that bale of cotton. Shoes were brought back for us all, Mist'ess got a dress, and the rest was brought back in money. I remember when we didn't have no gins, us little niggers would pick out the seed with our hands. My mother would card it; my grandma would spin it. Young Mist'ess was the weaver, and she made all our clothes. We just wore one garment, a long dress. The only way I could tell the difference in my sister's clothes and mine was mine had a little yoke on it.

We used to all go to the same church, colored and white. We would sit on one side. I would always go with my grandma. She would put her shoes in her pockets, and when we got in a mile of the church she put her shoes on. When we left, she would pull them off and go on home barefooted.

The preacher made my uncle Harry a deacon, and when they served bread and wine Uncle Harry would come down the aisle and pass it around. They had to break the ice to baptize. Uncle Harry's church was not up-to-date like they are now.

Us niggers had to have a pass anywhere we went, church and all. They never kept you from going anywhere, but you had to have that pass. There would be twenty-five white men who were called patterollers, and they would watch and could tell when one of the Negroes didn't have a pass; his feet just would not stay on the ground 'cause he was so nervous.

When we had big dances, the patterollers would be in the middle, us slaves would be on each end, and if the patterollers made a start to arrest one of the Negroes for disobedience we would always have a fire, and one of us would dip up a shovel of hot coals and throw it at them. By the time they got through dodging the hot coals, we would be gone home to our white folks.

Some of our happy days was when we hauled up the corn and we could swing on the wagons. They was sho' happy days. In slavery time, if any of the slaves was disobedient, their owners would hold them 'til the speculators came around. Then they was sold. If the women had children, it made no difference—they had to leave them. Or if the man had a wife, he had to go just the same.

I remember when the Yankees came through, one big Yankee come up to my pa and said, "I will give you my horse and blanket if you will show me all the old rich bugs [plantation owners]." Pa said, "Wait, let me get my shoes." Instead of putting on his shoes, he run through the house and yell, "Everybody turn loose the horses!" All the Yankees' horses were old broke-down horses, and they would take ours.

If a man wore a vest, the Yankees thought he had a watch. One big Yankee walked up to Uncle Harry and said, "Take off that vest." Another one said, "Let the damn fool alone. Can't you see he has no watch?" All the time, Uncle Harry had it hid under the woodpile. Just as soon as Uncle Harry got a chance, he threw his vest in the swamp.

One Yankee walked up to Mist'ess and said, "How come you got such a big bosom? Give me all that money." Mist'ess said, "I haven't got any money." The Yankee took his knife and cut Mist'ess's dress open, and gold and silver went everywhere. It was awful.

Mr. Franklin was my marster's older brother. The Yankees got him and hung him up by his toes. He would not tell where his money was. Then they hung him up by his neck. He could hardly whisper; still, he would not tell them where his money was. The Yankees yelled at one of his men to bring him the auger. He got poor old Mr. Franklin down and started boring in his head. Mr. Franklin said, "Please don't kill me. I will tell. It is under a pile of rocks in the garden in an old trunk." They got all of poor old Mr. Franklin's money.

We stuck to our marster and mist'ess. When they trusted their niggers, they would give them all their valuables to keep or hide for them. I can see one of the niggers on the place now. Marster gave him his watch to keep for him. He put it in his vest pocket. The chain stretched across his stomach. He walked out where the other niggers was, pretending they was Yankees. He rared back and put his fingers on his vest and said, "Now take it away from me like you would old Marster." He was so proud to get to wear his marster's watch.

The Yankees made my mother cook fifteen bushels of peas and three middlin's of meat. They didn't wait for them to get done. The peas just got hot and swelled. They took them and left with all the good horses they could catch of ours and all the money they could find.

If our marster and mist'ess saw a big, healthy nigger, it won't no trouble to get him married, for they would urge it on. It didn't make no difference, white or colored—if there was a wedding you could hear it all around. Everybody would go. We had straw brooms back in those days. One was fixed about the size around my arm, and five feet long. It was laid down on the floor. Everybody would gather around. The man and woman that was going to marry would stand by the broom. The preacher would say to the man, "Do you take this woman to be your wife?" He says, "Yes." "Well, jump the broom." After he jumped, the preacher would say the same to the woman. When she jumped, the preacher said, "I pronounce you man and wife." That's how all marriage ceremonies were then.

My young marster went to war to substitute for Mr. Franklin. It seems as if I can see him now. He called me

Ding. He said, "Here, Ding, take this big red apple, and if you don't ever see Marster again remember me by it." I never did see him no more. He got killed fighting. Mist'ess got forty dollars, but it was no good because we lost young Marster.

They called old John in to pray for Marster; he was a big nigger. His prayer was "God bless young Marster in the war, and give them their victory, and bless old Marster and Mist'ess at home." Going home, his wife, Mary, said, "John, how in the devil do you ever expect to be set free, and you praying like that?" Old John looked at Mary and said, "God knows what I mean."

Lord, them was some days.

I was ten years old [at the time of the surrender]. My father sent me to several different schools. We stayed on at the old plantation, though. My father and mother could stay together now, and they worked, and we had plenty. Lots of the old niggers were left without anything. My father would raise a bunch of hogs and put them in the cellar and sell them at a very high price. I can remember him selling wheat at sixty dollars a bushel. He made a pair of rawhide shoes one time and sold them for one hundred dollars to Mr. Ledbetter. My father cut down maple trees and let them dry. Then he made little pegs and used them for nails to make his shoes. He was a very smart man.

I kept going to school, walking fourteen miles every day, but I liked it, and I finally got my license and taught for several years.

I met a girl then and fell in love with her. Mr. Bob Yerby married Julia Johnson and me. We lived at New Grove, Georgia.

I decided that I wanted to give my work and soul to God. So I worked in the field by myself and picked three hundred pounds of cotton every day. I could chop three acres a day and make twelve bales of cotton and all the food I needed for my mule and cows. I took this and went to see about my studies for a preacher.

I studied theology under Dr. Lions and Dr. Clark. I can't remember when I joined the church, but it was over fifty years ago. I have lived in Clarke County all my life except ten years and have been a pastor for over twenty churches: Atlanta, Greene, Oglethorpe, Madison, Oconee, Jackson, Banks, Gwinnett Counties. I have baptized over three thousand people. God help me how many knots have I tied.

I lived on at New Grove. Julia and me had fourteen children—all good, healthy children. I stayed on 'til all the children died but five, and when Julia died I left New Grove. The children was grown anyway. I come to Athens, but I was pastor at Rome, Georgia. Willie, Sue, and Ophelis went to Richmond, Virginia. My oldest son died in Johnstown, Pennsylvania, during the World War. My other son lives here with me. He is a preacher, too. His church is at Allensville. Even though he is my son, I don't want to brag, but he is a very intelligent boy. As I have said, I am still pastor at Rome. I failed in health some, and I asked them to get another preacher, but they never have. I still go and preach when I can. I preached yesterday, and my text was the eighth chapter—the Psalm of David.

I have been a great man. When I walk in a church now, men draw up in knots. God breathed life in nostrils of man so we could do great things for Him.

Hannah Murphy

*Age 80 when interviewed
at her home in
Augusta, Georgia*

MY MOTHER BELONGED to Adam McNatt [the McNatt plantation was at a place then called Jefferson, near what is now Vidette], and my father belonged to Ponder. He had to get a pass to come see us, and he come Sundays and twice a week. All we chillun belonged to my mother's owner.

There was a big pond there, and I heard the old folks tell a story about that pond, how one time there was a white mist'ess what would go out every evening in her carriage and make the driver take her to the pond. She would stay out a long time, and the driver kept a-wondering what she did there. One night, he saw her go through bushes, and he crept up behind her. He saw her step out of her skin! The skin just rolled up and lay down on the ground, and then the mist'ess disappeared. The driver was too scared to move. He knelt there trembling, wondering what become of the mist'ess. In a little while, he heard her voice saying, "Skinny, skinny, don't you know me?" Her skin jumped up from the ground, and there she was again, as big as life! He watched her like that for a lot of nights, and it worried him. Pretty soon, he went and told the marster, and the marster was so scared of her he run her away from the plantation, and nobody ever saw her no more.

I seen many men running away from the bloodhounds. Sometimes we chillun be in the quarter playing, and a man would come running along fast, breathing hard, so scared! The hounds be behind him. Then I can remember how they'd whip them when they catch them. They would make the men drop down they pants and lay down across big logs, and they'd whip them. The womans, they'd drop they bodies, and they'd whip them across the back and around they waists 'til the blood come.

Us got food from the smokehouse. The old folks go there to get food once every week on what was called 'lowance night. They got bacon and meal. Sometimes they would have little gardens where they make truck. All I can 'member eating is just straight something to eat, no fancy eating—bread and meat and old black syrup. My mother and father was just straight field hands. Us had a log cabin, a dirt chimney put up out of clay, just one room to a family. Mother and her sister live in the same house. Chillun pretty much slept on the floor, and old folks had beds made out of boards nailed together with a rope cord strung across them instead of springs, and a cotton mattress over that.

They had not put me in the field to work. I was in the overseer's house, nursing his baby. I was nine years old when Freedom come, nursing Miss Ella Skinner's baby. Her husband was the overseer, named Jesse Skinner. They never whipped me 'cause I was too scared to do nothing wrong.

The old folks went to frolics, and they would give them a pass. They had fiddle, and all would dance. Sometimes the women held quilting. Us chillun played a lot of games, but I can 'member only one, call Mary Jane. You ring up and put yourself in a long line. Then you turn round and say, "Turn Jane!" Then everybody would sing,

> "Steal all down
> And don't slight none,
> Mary Jane.
> Turn round!
> Run down here,
> Turn all around,
> Don't slight none,
> Mary Jane."

I seen the patterollers, but I never heard no song about them. They was all white men. You want to go off your marster's place to another place, you had to get a pass from your bossman. If you didn't have that pass, the patterollers would whip you.

I'll never forget when the Yankees came through. They was singing "Dixie." They was all dressed in blue. They set the gin house afire, and then they went in the lot and got all the mules and the horses and carried them with them. They didn't bother the smokehouse, where the food was, and they didn't take no hogs. But they did go to the long dairy and throwed out all the milk and cream and butter and stuff. We chillun got in a bunch and looked at them. They didn't bother us none. The white folks heard they was coming, and they left. After the Yankees all gone away, the white folks came back. The colored folks stayed there awhile, but the owners of the place claimed they was free and sent the people off.

I know that my mother and father and a lot of the people come up here to Augusta. There was a long old shed, a kind of big house, where they stayed awhile. My father wanted to farm again. He went back down the country and worked for wages. He rented and worked farm 'til he died.

Fannie Coleman
*Interviewed at her home
in Toccoa, Georgia in 1937*

I BELONGED TO Marse Chesley Cawthon. He had
three sons: Larkin, Chesley, and Tom, all dead now. I
had three chillun, too. They're all dead. I was born in
Virginny. 'Bout the first thing I recollects is being put
up on the block and sold 'long with Granny and a young
boy. I weren't so very old, 'cause I didn't have but two
teeth. Guess I was 'bout six years old.

Next thing I knowed, my folks was living at
Spartanburg, South Carolina. Then they come to Georgia. I belonged to Marse Jesse Walters, then to Marse
Joe Vickery, before Marse Chesley bought me. When I
went to him, he lived in Franklin County 'bout four
miles from Carnesville. Then he moved up here. He

had a good deal of land. From where the Larkin Cawthon place is way back towards Currahee, all them hills and valleys belonged to him. I don't know how many hundred acres, but there was a lot of it.

I used to card and spin. Us used to spin and weave our clothes in them days. I worked in the fields, too. I'd get up and get breakfast, milk and churn, and be in the field an hour by sunup. We quit 'bout sundown to get home and have time to feed and milk and do things for night. I had my bed in the kitchen. I'd get up and make fires. My white folks had a big house, and the kitchen was off to itself.

I loves to hear any preaching. I belonged to the Baptist Church first, then I joined the Methodist with my husband. I was married 'fore I was free by Steve Jackson, a colored preacher. I married Henry Coleman, who belonged to Marse George Crawford from down 'bout Carnesville, and my white folks bought Henry for me after we married.

The Cawthons had two women servants and me and Henry, that was all. When any of us was sick, they give us some sort of tea.

I can't read and write. Old-time folks ain't got no learning. Young folks now got all the learning; sometimes I think they got too much learning.

Emma Coker
Interviewed in
Augusta, Georgia

MY BROTHER CAN TELL YOU, my grandfather was a red Injun, and my father was a black Injun—a cross. That's why we-all got so much red blood. My hair used to be long like an Injun's, but it curled up after I got old.

I work at the Riverside Mill more than twenty years, and I'll never be the workhorse I was. I can still nurse good, but I ain't able to go out yet. White folks sho' is kind to me. I gets this little house for nothing, and they bring me food. I hopes to get a pension.

I only had one chile. I had him when I was too young to know nothing 'bout childbirth, and my mama done everything for me. The boy was born stillborn, but the doctor spank him and make him cry up. I marked him with a rabbit! There was a lady had pretty rabbits near me, regular pets they was, and she promise to sell me one. I sho' did love 'em; I watch 'em every day. And then she went and sold 'em to a lady! I grieve 'bout that little rabbit and mark my boy, and he got that mark yet. But he don't 'low me to tell whereabout it is.

Ain't you never seen nobody with a mark dat-a-way? My sister had a baby mark with wild blackberry roll on its back—a perfect roll just like colored folks make. Another of my sisters mark her baby with a pig feet. She saw some pig feet through the crack of the fence. It mark the baby, look just as natural as if it was sure-enough pig feet, just as pretty!

None of my sister's chillun give her the hereafter pains, 'cause she knowed what to do. They say them is harder than havin' a chile. She had a heap of chillun and always took a meal bag and put it right in the span of her back and lay down on it, and it takes off all the hereafter pains.

If you plant a vegetable garden when a chile is born, and you walk through it before the chile is growed like it oughta, the chile will die. They say if you get good and mad sure enough and run out right away and sow pepper, you'll get more peppers than you want. Put a penny round the ankle for rheumatiz. Drink water from the trough where the horse been drinkin' and you cures a lot of germs. I've seen 'em did that. Best to let yo' mole stay on your face; you get cancer if you take it off. When white folks done that, they dies. Fig-leaf juice good for ringworms; just break the leaf and let the milk run on it. If you can get green walnuts, cut 'em and let the milk get on the ringworms; it'll cure 'em every time. I cure acute indigestion with mustard and salt and hot water. For a cross-eyed baby, every time the chile look up at you, rub yo' hand down his face, and that'll straighten his eyes. Chicken gizzards hanged up 'til they is dry and made into tea is good for teething. If you get a nail in yo' foot, just put some fat meat on it and a penny. If you can't get the penny, put the meat on it, and it'll heal up.

I don't want 'em to take me to no undertaker. They says if you seen what they does to dead folks, you wouldn't want 'em to draw the blood from you. Best to stick a piece of cotton up each side of the nose, dip it in turpentine and salt; that keeps the blood from comin' out. Take salt and turpentine and put it right under the board or lay it on the breast, and the body will keep as long as the undertaker can keep it. Throw away the comb and brush of the dead person; it will be bad luck for anybody to use it. Burn up the dead people's clothes and any clothes what is got bad odor. Anything you die in is rank poison; you must burn 'em up. Why, there was a woman who had a sweetheart on the side and used to give him things she buy with her husband's money. The husband die of smallpox, and the sweetheart craved his fine clothes, so the woman give 'em to the sweetheart. Everybody say, "You goin' catch that!" but he say, "They is fine clothes, and I wants 'em." And sho' enough, the sweetheart die of smallpox, too.

I hates to talk about haints, 'cause they come to see you at night if you talk 'bout 'em in the daytime. A woman come to my son's store, ask him for old shoes. He say, "Old lady, is you a root doctor?" She say, "No, I just wants to burn 'em on Friday." I guess she wanted to drive haints away, but he wouldn't give her none.

The haints come in my window sometimes. I saw a man; sometimes they look like a woman, sometimes like little babies. You got to pray hard so they will go away. Sometimes they come in over the door and sometimes by the window, and they cackle like chicken but don't never talk none to me. They try to cover you up. I gets up and get to fightin' 'em and run 'em out. On rainy nights, they come in. If you talk 'bout them, you'll see 'em tonight. I tried putting matches in my hair to keep 'em away. One white lady that is so good to me, she give me a string of beads with a cross on it, and I use that, but the minister heard about it, and he said I mustn't use it; that is like serving two religions.

All you got to do is cut off a piece of tail and bury it under the front steps, and you can keep yo' cat or dog at home. They say if you wants to keep yo' chickens at home, put chamber lye in their water, and they never go away from home. If you cuts out a dress on Friday, it ain't likely you'll finish it. Nobody like to carry their sewin' round on Friday; they never get it done. I have seen people put a rusty nail in chicken water to make the fowl tender, and have seen 'em take a broken plant and cook the chicken with it in the pot. Bad luck to break off a piece of bread in another person's hand. Bad luck to sit on a table or to sweep the table off. It's bad luck to swing a chair round on one leg. You mustn't rock a chair if the chile in it has gone to sleep. And two lamps burnin' in one room is a sho' sign of death. If you burn a lamp all night, they say you is burnin' daylight; but I do that 'cause I gets nervous like at night. Bad luck to sing while you eat and after you get to bed. I burn up my hair combings; if the birds get it, make a nest of it, it make you have a toothache. If a kinky-headed nigger touch the head of a straight-haired person, the straight hair falls out. But if the straight-haired person combs the kinks out of a nigger's head, that make it grow.

I have looked in the well, and it is my belief it told me true. I never looked but once; I never want to see no more what I seen then. I seen my mother's death. I seen a woman in a coffin, dressed in a beautiful white dress. She had a cross on her breast all tangled round with stars. Look like she was walkin' on the clouds.

Marshal Butler
Age 88
when interviewed in 1937

I IS EIGHTY-EIGHT YEARS OLD and was born on December 25. I know it was Christmas Day, for I was a gift to my folks. Anyhow, I is the only nigger that knows exactly how old he is. I don't remember the year, but you white folks can figure it out.

My mammy was Harriet Butler, and my pappy was John Butler, and we was all raised in Washington-Wilkes. Mammy was a Frank Collar nigger, and her man was of the tribe of Ben Butler, some miles down the road. It was one of them trial marriages; they tried so hard to see each other, but old Ben Butler said two passes a week was enough to see my mammy on the Collar plantation. When the war was completed, Pappy came home to us. We was a family of ten—four females called Sally, Liza, Ellen, and Lottie and six strong bucks called Charlie, Elisha, Marshal, Jack, Heywood, and little Johnnie, the baby.

The Collar plantation was big, and I don't know the size of it. It must have been big, for there was 250 niggers aching to go to work; I guess they must have been aching after the work was done. Marse Frank bossed the place hisself—there were no overseers. We raised cotton, corn, wheat, and everything we ate. There was no market to bring the goods to. Marse Frank was like a foodal [feudal] lord of history, as my good-for-nothing grandson would say. He is the one with book learning from Atlanta. Waste of time filling up a nigger's head with that trash. What that boy needs is muscle-ology—just look at my head and hands.

My mammy was a maid in the Collars' home, and she had many fine dresses; some of them were given to her by her missus. Pappy was a field nigger for old Ben Butler, and I worked in the field when I was knee high to a grasshopper. We ate our breakfast while it was dark, and we trooped to the fields at sunup, carrying our lunch with us—nothing fancy, but just good rib-sticking vittles. We come in from the fields at sundown, and there was a good meal awaiting us in the slave quarters. My good marster give out rations every second Monday, and all day Monday was taken to separate the wheat from the chaff—that is, I mean the vittles had to be organized to be marched off to the proper depository.

Marse Frank gave Mammy four acres of ground to till for herself and us children. We raised cotton—yes, sir! One bale of it and lots of garden truck. Our bossman give us Saturday as a holiday to work our four acres.

All the niggers worked hard. The cotton pickers had to pick two hundred pounds of cotton a day, and if a nigger didn't Marse Frank would take the nigger to the barn and beat him with a switch. He would tell the nigger to holler loud as he could, and the nigger would do so. Then the old mist'ess would come in and say, "What are you doing, Frank?" "Beating a nigger" would be his answer. "You let him alone. He is my nigger." And both Marse Frank and the whipped nigger would come out of the barn. We all loved Marse and Mist'ess. No, we was never whipped for stealing. We never stole anything in those days—much.

We sure frolicked Saturday nights. That was our day to howl, and we howled. Our gals sure could dance, and when we was thirsty we had lemonade and whiskey. No, sir, we never mixed whiskey with water. Those that wanted lemonade got it; the gals all liked it. Niggers never got drunk those days; we was scared of the patterollers. A fiddle and a tin can, and one nigger would beat his hand on the can, and another nigger would beat the strings on the fiddle with broom straws. It was almost like a banjo. I remember we sung "Little Liza Jane" and "Green Grows the Willow Tree." The frolic broke up in the morning—about two o'clock—and we all scattered to whichever way we was going.

We put on clean clothes on Sunday and went to church. We went to the white church. Us niggers sat on one side, and the white folks sat on the other. We was baptized in the church; the "pool room" was right in the church.

If we went visiting, we had to have a pass. If a nigger went out without a pass, the patterollers would get him. The white folks were the patterollers and had masks on their faces. The looked like niggers with the devil in their eyes. They used no paddles—nothing but straps with the belt buckle fastened on.

Yes, sir, I got paddled. It happened this way. I left home on Thursday to see a gal on the Palmer plantation, five miles away. I didn't get no pass—the boss was so busy! Everything was fine until my return trip. I was two miles out and three miles to go. There come the patterollers. I was not scared, only I couldn't move. They give me thirty licks. I ran the rest of the way home. There was belt buckles all over me. I ate my vittles off the porch railing. It was worth that paddlin' to see that gal. I would do it over again to see Mary the next night.

We niggers were a healthy lot. If we was really sick, Marse Frank would send for Dr. Fielding Ficklin of Washington. If it was just a small cold, the nigger would go to the woods and get catnip and roots and such things. If it was a tummy ache, there was the castor oil. The white folks say children cry for it; I done my cryin' afterwards. For sore throat, there was alum. Everybody made their own soap. If a hand was burned, you would use soap as a poultice and place it on the hand. If you cut your finger, you used kerosene with a rag around it. Turpentine was for sprains and bad cuts. For constipation, we used tea made from sheep droppings. And if you're away from home, the speed of the feet do not match the speed of this remedy.

I am not superstitious, and I believe in no signs. I just carry a rabbit's foot for luck. But I do believe the screeching of an owl is a sign of death. I found it to be true. I had an uncle named Haywood. He stayed at my house and was sick for a month but wasn't so bad off. One night, Uncle had a relapse, and that same night a screech owl come along and sat on the top of the house, and he—I mean the owl—*whoo*ed three times, and next morning Uncle got worse, and at eleven o'clock he died.

I do believe in signs. When the rooster crows in the house, it is a sign of a stranger coming. If foot itches, you is going to walk on strange land. If a cow lows at a house at night, death will be round the house in short time. If sweeping out ashes at night, that is bad luck, for you is sweeping out your best friend. Remember, your closest friend is your worst enemy.

If you wanted to go a-courtin', it would take a week or so to get your gal. Sometimes some fool nigger would bring a gal a present—like pulled candy and such like. I had no time for such foolishness. You would pop the question to the bossman to see if he was willing for you to marry the gal. There was no minister or bossman to marry you—no limitations at all. Bossman would just say, "Don't forget to bring me a little one or two for next year." The bossman would fix a cottage for two, and there you was established for life.

Marse Frank had plenty of visitors to see him, and his three gals was excuse for anyone for miles around to come trompin' in. He entertained mostly on Tuesday and Thursday nights. I remembers them nights, for what was left over from the feasts the niggers would eat. Dr. Fielding Ficklin, Bill Pope, Judge Reese, General Robert Toombs, and Alexander Stephens from Crawfordville—all would come to Marse Frank's big house.

General Robert Toombs lived in Washington and had a big plantation 'bout a mile from the city. He was a farmer, and very rich. The general was a big man—'bout six feet tall, heavy, and had a full face. He always had unlighted cigar in his mouth. He was the first man I saw who smoked ten-cent cigars. Niggers use to run to get the stumps, and the lucky nigger who got the stump could even sell it for a dime to the other niggers. For after all, wasn't it General Toombs' cigar? The general never wore expensive clothes and always carried a crooked-handled walking stick. I never heard him say "nigger," never heard him cuss. He always helped us niggers—gave us nickels and dimes at times.

I saw a red cloud in the west in 1860. I knew war was brewing. Marse Frank went to war. My uncle was his man and went to war with him. Uncle brought him back after the battle at Gettysburg—wounded. He died later. My mistress and her boys ran the plantation.

The bluecoats came to our place in '62 and '63. They took everything that was not red-hot or nailed down. The war made no changes; we did the same work and had plenty to eat.

The war was now over. We didn't know we was free until a year later. I stayed on with Marse Frank's boys for twenty years. I did the same work for thirty-five to forty dollars a year, with rations thrown in.

I lived so long because I tell no lies. I never spent more than fifty cents for a doctor in my life. I believe in whiskey, and that kept me goin'. And let me tell you, I'm always going to be a nigger 'til I die.

Lula Flannigan
Age 78 when interviewed

THEY SAYS I WAS JUST FOUR years old when the war was over, but I sure does 'member that day them Yankee soldiers come down the road. Mary and Willie Durham was my mammy and pappy, and they belong to Marse Spence Durham at Watkinsville in slavery times.

When word come that the Yankee soldiers was on the way, Marse Spence and his sons was away at the war. Miss Betsey told my pappy to take and hide the horses down in the swamp. My mammy help Miss Betsey sew up the silver in the cotton bed ticks. Them Yankee soldiers never did find our white folks' horses and their silver.

Miss Marzee, she was Marse Spence and Miss Betsey's daughter. She was playing on the pianny when the Yankee soldiers come down the road. Two soldiers come in the house and ask her to play a tune that they liked. I forget the name of their tune. Miss Marzee gets up from the pianny, and she 'low that she ain't going to play no tune for no Yankee men. Then the soldiers take her out and set her up top of the high gatepost in front of the big house and make her set there 'til the whole regiment pass by. She set there and cried, but she sure ain't never played no tune for them Yankee men.

The Yankee soldiers took all the blankets off the beds. They stole all the meat they wanted from the smokehouse. They bashed in the top of the syrup barrels and then turn the barrels upside down.

Marse Spence gave me to Miss Marzee to be her own maid, but slavery time ended before I was big enough to be much good to her.

Us had lots better times them days than now. Whatever these niggers know 'bout corn shuckin's and log rollin's and house raisin's? Marse Spence used to let his niggers have candy pullin's in syrup-makin' time, and the way us would dance in the moonlight was something these niggers nowadays don't know nothing 'bout.

All the white folks love to see plenty of healthy, strong black chillun coming 'long, and they was watchful to see that women had good care when they chillun was borned. They let these women do easy, light work towards the last before the chillun is borned, and then afterwards they don't do nothing much 'til they is well and strong again. Folks tell 'bout some plantations where the women would run back home from the field and have their baby, and then they'd be back in the field swinging a hoe before night that same day, but there weren't nothing like that round Watkinsville.

When a screech owl holler at night, us put an iron in the fire quick, and then us turned all the shoes upside down on the floor and turned the pockets wrong side out on all the clothes, because if they didn't do them things quick something mighty bad was sure to happen. Most likely, somebody going to be dead in that house before long, if us weren't quick about fixing. What us do in summertime about fire at night for the screech owl? Us just uncovered the coals in the fireplace.

Us didn't have no matches, and us banked the fire with ashes every night all the year round. If the fire go out because some nigger got careless about it, then somebody got to go off to the next plantation sometime to get live coals. Some of them men could work the flints right good, but that was a hard job. They just rub them flint rocks together right fast and let the sparks they make drape down on a piece of punk wood, and they get a fire that way if they is lucky.

Them days, nobody bring an ax in the house on his shoulder. That was a sure sign of bad luck. And never lay no broom across the bed. One time, a likely pair of black folks get married, and somebody give them a new broom. The woman, she was proud of her nice spanking-new broom, and she lay it on the bed for the wedding crowd to see it, with other things been give 'em. For three years, her man was beating her, and not long after that she go plumb stark crazy. She ought to know better than to lay their broom on her bed. It sure done brung her bad luck. They sent her off to the crazy folks' place, and she died there.

I WAS BORN on a plantation in Bibb County between Clinton and Macon. Marster's name was William Wolfolk, so that made my mother's name Patsy Wolfolk and my daddy's Green Wolfolk. Marster was rich and had a-plenty. He and his folks lived in a big house in Macon, but he come out regular to see 'bout his land and niggers. I reckon maybe he had 'bout three hundred hands, 'cause the plantation was just full of niggers. Marster had a white man on the place that was a overseer. He lived in a big house with all the nigger cabins kinder back of it, yet his house was in the middle of them. I could find that old plantation right now if I could just get that far up the country.

The women on the place never done work so much but raise chillun. Ma had fourteen, but she helped weave and dye the cloth, too. The women tended to the chillun well, saw that they had plenty milk and greens and meat and bread, and then when bedtime come they was put to bed clean.

My daddy was a blacksmith. He sho' was smart. There wasn't but two on the place, and my daddy'd take the young boys and learn them the trade.

When I got big enough, I was the house girl for the overseer's folks. I swept the floors and washed the dishes and did what Missie told me to. I called the overseer's wife Missie. When they got through eatin', I ate and had a-plenty. We didn't have to go off from home to borrow nothin'. I wish things was like they was then; they took care of they niggers.

On the Fourth of July and Christmas, too, Marster give us a big time. Fourth of July was just like a weddin'. We always had a big dinner and could invite some of our friends to come, but the company and all of us had to behave. There wasn't no runnin' off stealin' and fightin'. When the company left, they left without a blemish. Sometimes Marster'd give us candy pullin's and quiltin's.

Marster was a good man hisself and wanted all his niggers to be good. Right there on the place, he had a church built for us. He was a Baptist, so we was Baptists. We had preachin' every Sunday mornin' and Sunday school for the chillun Sunday afternoon. When a nigger joined the church, there sho' was a lot of shoutin' and singin'. Wish you coulda heard it. Then he was baptized in a pond right there on the place with ever'body shoutin'. A colored preacher did the baptizin'. When the shoutin' would quiet down a little, they'd sing "Jesus and I All to Heaven Are Goin'."

Marster had his niggers where they'd mind good. He never let no patterollers on the place, and he never let the overseer whip them. When he told them to work, he meant for them to work, and they knowed it. He never let them run around all over the country like they does nowadays.

Folks was married by a colored preacher, and they stayed right there at home and worked. The boys married the gals that was raised right there on the plantation. Marster had his rule, and they all stuck by it. They weren't no big weddin's, and folks was more peaceable and quiet than they is now.

Ever'thing in God's world that the niggers wanted, Marster had right there on the place. Had plenty shoes and clothes and somethin' to eat, and that's all we needed. I know Marster went to heaven 'cause he was so good to us.

Yankees come to Eatonton one mornin' at daybreak and tore it up. From there, they come to the plantation. We had done all hid ever'thing we could. The fine mules and other stock was hid in the woods, and the silver and other valuables was buried. All the meat and syrup and lard was locked up in the smokehouse. We'd done heard how they tore up other places, and we was scared.

I was goin' from the backyard to the kitchen when they come. I had a fork in my hand. They saw me, and one of the Yankees said, "Halt," and I halt. He said, "Where you goin'?" I said, "To take this to Missie." He said, "You ain't got no Missie. You is free." I said, "I is goin' to take this to Missie," and I did.

Then they began tearing up everything. They found the fine mules and took them and left us they sorry ones. They scared some of the niggers so bad that they up and told where ever'thing was hid. I never told nothin'. They busted open the smokehouse and got all the meat and lard and syrup. They took the dishes and ever'thing they wanted out of the kitchen, and I screamed and hollered. Didn't do no good; they took it anyhow. They even took some of the young boys with them, and we ain't never saw them no more.

Soon as ever'thing got quieted down, Marster come out there and got us all together. He told us we was free, but as long as he had bread he'd keep as many as wanted to stay. Most ever'body stayed right there for two or three years. We stayed three years, and then Pa died, so we live with my married sister. She married a man that loved to ramble, so we just moved round the country for a long time.

I used to see old Marster as long as we was livin' in Bibb County, but when we got way off I never seen him no more. My sister's husband got killed, and after that we just roamed from place to place. I married before I came to Hawkinsville, but I been here 'bout twenty-seven years. I lost my husband and most of my chillun right here. But now that I'm old, I want to go back home. I know most of the old white folks is dead, but I want to go home.

Rachel Adams
*Age 78 when interviewed
in Athens, Georgia*

THAT'S BEEN SUCH A LONG TIME back that I has 'most forgot how things went. Anyhow, I was born in Putnam County 'bout two miles from Eatonton, Georgia. My ma and pa was 'Melia and Isaac Little, and far as I know they was born and bred in that same county. Pa, he was sold away from me when I was still a baby. Ma's job was to weave all the cloth for the white folks. I have wore many a dress made out of the homespun that she wove. There was seventeen of us chillun, and I can't 'member the name of but two of 'em now—they was John and Sarah. John was Ma's onliest son; all the rest of the other sixteen of us was gals.

Us lived in mud-daubed log cabins what had old

stick chimneys made out of sticks and mud. Our old homemade bed didn't have slats or metal springs neither. They used stout cords for springs. The cloth what they made the tick of them old hay mattresses and pillows out of was so coarse that it scratched us little chillun 'most to death, it seemed like to us them days. I can still feel them old hay mattresses under me now. Every time I moved at night, it sounded like the wind blowin' through them peach trees and bamboos round the front of the house where I lives now.

Grandma Anna was 115 years old when she died. She done wore herself out in slavery time. Grandpa, he was sold off somewhere. Both of them was field hands.

Potlikker and cornbread was fed to us chillun out of big old wooden bowls. Two or three chillun ate out of the same bowl. Grown folks had meat, greens, syrup, cornbread, taters, and the like. Possums! I should say so. They catch plenty of them, and after they was killed Ma would scald 'em and rub 'em in hot ashes, and that cleaned 'em just as pretty and white. Ooh, but they was good. They used to go fishin' and rabbit huntin', too. Us just fetched in game galore then, for it was the style them days. There wasn't no market meat in slavery days. Seemed like to me in them days that ash-roasted taters and ground peas was the best something to eat what anybody could want. Course, they had a garden, and it had somethin' of just about everything what us knowed anything 'bout in the way of garden sass growin' in it. All the cooking was done in them big old oven fireplaces what was fixed up special for the pots and ovens.

Summertime, us just wore homespun dresses made like the slips they use for underwear now. The coats what us wore over our wool dresses in winter was knowed as "sacks" then, 'cause they was so loose fittin'. They was heavy and had wool in 'em, too. Marse Lewis, he had plenty of sheep, 'cause they was bound to have lots of warm winter clothes. And then, too, they liked mutton to eat. Oh! Them old brogan shoes was coarse and rough. When Marse Lewis had a cow killed, they put the hide in the tannin' vat. When the hide was ready, Uncle Ben made up the shoes, and sometimes they let Uncle Jasper help him if there was many to be made all at one time. Us wore the same sort of clothes on Sunday as every day, only they had to be clean and fresh when they was put on Sunday mornin'.

Marse Lewis Little and his wife, Miss Sallie, owned us, and old Miss, she died long 'fore the surrender. Marse Lewis, he was right good to all his slaves, but that overseer, he would beat us down in a minute if us didn't do to suit him. When they give slaves tasks to do and they weren't done in a certain time, that old overseer would whip 'em 'bout that. Marster never had to take none of his niggers to court or put 'em in jails neither; him and the overseer set 'em right. Long as Miss Sallie lived, the carriage driver drove her and Marse Lewis around, but after she died there weren't so much use of the carriage. He just drive for Marse Lewis and piddled around the yard then.

Some slaves learned to read and write.

If they went to meetin', they had to go with their

white folks, 'cause they didn't have no separate churches for the niggers 'til after the war. On our marster's place, slaves didn't go off to meetin' at all. They just went round to one another's houses and sung songs. Some of 'em read the Bible by heart. Once, I heared a man preach what didn't know how to read one word in the Bible, and he didn't even have no Bible yet.

The first baptizin' I ever seen was after I was right 'bout grown. If a slave from our place ever joined up with a church before the war was over, I never heard nothin' 'bout it.

I didn't know nothin' 'bout what a funeral was, them days. If a nigger died that mornin', they sure didn't waste no time a-puttin' him right on down in the ground that same day. Them coffins never had no shape to 'em; they was just squared pine boxes. Now wasn't that terrible?

Slaves never went nowhere without them patterollers beatin' 'em up if they didn't have no pass.

There was hundreds of acres in that there plantation. Marse Lewis had a heap of slaves. The overseer, he had a bugle what he blowed to wake up the slaves. He blowed it long 'fore day, so that they could eat breakfast and be out there in the fields waitin' for the sun to rise, so they could see how to work. And they stayed out there and worked 'til black dark. When a rainy spell come and the grass get to growin' fast, they worked them slaves at night, even when the moon wasn't shining. On them nights, one set of slaves held lanterns for the others to see how to chop the weeds out of the cotton and corn. Work was sure tight in them days. Every slave had a task to do after they got back to them cabins at night. They each one had to spin their stint same as the women, every night.

Young and old washed their clothes Saturday nights. They hardly knowed what Sunday was. They didn't have but one day in the Christmas, and the only difference they saw that day was that they give 'em biscuits on Christmas Day. New Year's Day was rail-splittin' day. They was told how many rails was to be cut, and them niggers better split that many or somebody was going to get beat up.

I don't remember much 'bout what us played, 'cept the way us run round in a ring. Us chillun was always scared to play in the thicket nigh the house 'cause Raw Head and Bloody Bones lived there.

They used to scare us 'bout red taters. They was fine taters, red on the outside and pretty and white on the inside, but white folks called 'em "nigger killers." That was one of their tricks to keep us from stealin' them taters. There wasn't nothin' wrong with them taters; they was just as good and healthy as any other taters. Aunt Lucy, she was the cook, and she told me that slaves was scared of them nigger-killer taters and never bothered them much then, like they does the yam patches these days.

I used to think I saw haints at night, but it always turned out to be somebody that was tryin' to scare me.

'Bout the most fun slaves had was at them corn shuckin's. The general would get high up on top of the corn pile and whoop and holler down, leadin' that corn-shuckin' song 'til all the corn was done shucked. Then come the big eats, the liquor, and the dancin'. Cotton pickin's was big fun, too, and when they got through pickin' the cotton they ate and drank and danced 'til they couldn't dance no more.

White folks just had to be good to sick slaves, 'cause slaves was property. For old Marster, to lose a slave was losin' money. There weren't so many doctors them days, and homemade medicines was all the go. Oil and turpentine, camphor, asafiddy [asafetida], cherry bark, sweet gum bark—all them things was used to make teas for grown folks to take for their ailments. Red oak bark tea was given to chillun for stomach miseries.

All I can recollect 'bout the comin' of Freedom was old Marster tellin' us that us was free as jack rabbits and that from then on niggers would have to get their own somethin' to eat. It wasn't long after that when them Yankees with pretty blue clothes on came through our place, and they stole 'most everything our marster had. They killed his chickens, hogs, and cows and took his horses off and sold 'em. That didn't look right, did it?

My aunt give us a big weddin' feast when I married Tom Adams, and she sure did pile up that table with heaps of good eats. My weddin' dress was blue, trimmed in white. Us had six chillun, nine grandchillun, and nineteen great-grandchillun. One of my grandchillun has done been blind since he was three weeks old. I sent him off to the blind school, and now he can get around least as good as I can. He has made his home with me ever since his mammy died.

'Cordin' to my way of thinkin', Abraham Lincoln done a good thing when he set us free. Jeff Davis, he was all right, too, 'cause if him and Lincoln hadn't got to fightin', us would have been slaves to this very day. It's mighty good to do just as you please, and bread and water is heaps better than that somethin' to eat us had to slave for.

I joined up with the church 'cause I wanted to go to Heaven when I dies, and if folks live right they sure is going to have a good restin' place in the next world. I sure believe in religion, that I does.

I WAS BORNED on Marster Joe Echols' plantation in Oglethorpe County, 'bout ten miles from Lexington, Georgia. Mammy was Cynthia Echols 'fore she married up with my daddy. He was Peyton Shepherd. After Pappy and Mammy got married, old Marse Shepherd sold Pappy to Marse Echols so as they could stay together.

Marse Joe, he had three plantations, but he didn't live on one of 'em. He lived in Lexington. He kept an overseer on each one of his plantations, and they had better be good to his niggers or else Marse Joe would sure get 'em away from there. He never 'lowed 'em to work us too hard, and in bad or real cold weather us didn't have to do no outside work except everyday chores what had to be done come rain or shine, like milkin', tendin' the stock, fetchin' in wood, and things like that. He saw that us had plenty of good something to eat and all the clothes us needed. Us was lots better off in them days than us is now.

Old Marster, he had so many niggers that he never knowed 'em all. One day, he was a-ridin' 'long towards one of his plantations and he met one of his slaves, named William. Marse Joe stopped him and asked him who he was. William said, "Why, Marster, I'm your nigger. Don't you know me?" Then Marster, he just laughed and said, "Well, hurry on home when you gets what you is going after." He was in a good humor that way 'most all of the time. I can see him now a-ridin' that little hoss of his what he called Button, and his little fice dog hoppin' 'long on three legs right 'side of the hoss. There wasn't nothing the matter with that little dog; walkin' on three legs was just his way of getting round.

Marster never let none of the slave chillun on his plantation do no work until they got fifteen—that was soon enough, he said. On all of his plantation, there was one old woman that didn't have nothin' else to do but look after and cook for the nigger chillun whilst they mammies was at work in the fields. Aunt Viney took care of us. She had a big old horn that she blowed when it was time for us to eat, and us knowed better than to get so far off us couldn't hear that horn, for Aunt Viney would sure tear us up. Marster had done told her she better fix us plenty to eat and give it to us on time. There was a great, long trough what went plumb 'cross the yard, and that was where us ate. For dinner, us had peas or some other sort of vegetable and cornbread. Aunt Viney crumbled up that bread in the trough and poured the vegetables and potlikker over it. Then she blowed the horn, and chillun come a-runnin' from every which way. If us ate it all up, she had to put more vittles in the trough. At nights, she crumbled the cornbread in the trough and poured buttermilk over it. Us never had nothin' but cornbread and buttermilk at night. Sometimes that trough would be a sight 'cause us never stopped to wash our hands, and 'fore us had been eatin' more than a minute or two what was in the trough would look like the red mud what had come off our hands. Sometimes Aunt Viney would fuss us and make us clean it out.

There was a big sand bar down on the crick what made a fine place to play, and wadin' in the branches was lots of fun. Us frolicked up and down them woods and had all sorts of good times—anything to keep away from Aunt Viney, 'cause she was sure to have us fetchin' in wood or sweepin' the yard if us was handy where she could find us. If us was out of her sight, she never bother 'bout them yards and things. Us was scared to answer that horn when us got in Marster's 'bacco. He raised lots of 'bacco and rationed it out to men, but he never 'lowed chillun to have none 'til the day they was big enough to work in the fields. Us found out how to get in his 'bacco house, and us kept on gettin' his 'bacco 'fore it was dried out, 'til he missed it. Then he told Aunt Viney to blow that horn and call up all the chillun.

"I am going to whip every one of 'em," he would declare. After us got there and he saw that green 'bacco had done made us so sick us couldn't eat, he just couldn't beat us. He just laughed and said, "It's good enough for you."

Aunt Martha, she done the milkin' and helped Aunt Nancy cook for the slaves. They had a big, long kitchen up at the big house, where the overseer lived. The slaves that worked in the field never had to do their own cookin'. It was all done for 'em in that big old kitchen. Them cooks knowed they had to cook a-plenty and have it ready when it was time for the slaves to come in from the fields. Miss Ellen—she was the overseer's wife—went out in the kitchen and looked over everything to see that it was all right, and then she blowed the bugle. When the slaves heard that bugle, they come in a-singin' from the fields. They was happy 'cause they knowed Miss Ellen had a good dinner ready for 'em.

There weren't many folks sick them days, 'specially 'mongst the slaves. When one did die, folks would go twelve or fifteen miles to the buryin'. Marster would say, "Take the mules and wagons and go, but mind you, take good care of them mules." He never seemed to care if us went—fact was, he said us ought to go. If a slave died on our place, nobody went to the fields 'til after the buryin'. Marster never let nobody be buried 'til they had been dead twenty-four hours, and if they had people from some other place he waited 'til they could get there. He said it wasn't right to hurry 'em off into the ground too quick after they died.

There wasn't no undertakers them days. The home folks just laid the corpse out on the coolin' board 'til the coffin was made. A coolin' board was made out of a long, straight plank raised a little at the head, and had legs fixed to make it set straight. They wrapped women's corpses in windin' sheets. Uncle Squire, the man what done all the wagon work and buildin' on our place, made the coffins. They was just plain wood boxes they painted to make 'em look nice. White preachers conducted the funerals, and most of the time our own marster done it, 'cause he was a preacher himself. When the funeral was done preached, they sung "Harps from the Tomb." Then they put the coffin in a wagon and drive slow and careful to the graveyard. The preacher prayed at the grave, and the mourners sung "I's Born to Die and Lay This Body Down." They never had no outside box for the coffin to be set in, but they put planks on top of the coffin 'fore they started shovelin' in the dirt.

Fourth Sundays was our meetin' days, and everybody went to church. Us went to our white folks' church and rode in a wagon behind their carriage. There was two Baptist preachers. One of 'em was Mr. John Gibson, and the other was Mr. Patrick Butler. Marse Joe was a Methodist preacher himself, but they all went to the same church together. The niggers sat in the gallery. When they had done given the white folks the sacrament, they called the niggers down from the gallery and give them sacrament, too. Church days was sure enough big meetin' days, 'cause everybody went. They preached three times a day—at eleven in the mornin', at three in the evenin', and then again at night. The biggest meetin' house was when they had baptizin', and that was right often. They dammed up the crick on Saturday so as it would be deep enough on Sunday, and they done the baptizin' 'fore they preached the three o'clock sermon. At them baptizin's, there was all sorts of shoutin', and they would sing "Roll, Jordan, Roll," "The Livin' Waters," and "Lord, I's Comin' Home."

When the crops was laid by and most of the hardest work of the year done, then was camp meetin' time, 'long in the last of July and sometimes in August. That was when us had the biggest times of all. They had great big long tables and just everything good to eat. Marster would kill five or six hogs and have 'em carried there to be barbecued, and he carried all his cooks along. After the white folks ate, they fed the niggers, and there was always plenty for all. Marster sure looked after all his niggers good at them times. When the camp meetin' was over, then come the big baptizin'—white folks first, then niggers. One time, there was a old slave woman what got so scared when they got her out in the creek that somebody had to pull her feet out from under her to get her under the water. She got out from there and testified that it was the devil a-holdin' her back.

The white ladies had nice silk dresses to wear to church. Slave women had new calico dresses what they wore with hoop skirts they made out of grapevines. They work poke bonnets with ruffles on 'em, and if the weather was sort of cool they wore shawls. Marster always wore his linen duster. That was his white coat, made cutaway style with long tails.

The cloth for 'most all of the clothes was made at home. Marse Joe raised lots of sheep, and the wool was used to make cloth for the winter clothes. Us had a great, long loom house where some of the slaves didn't do nothin' but weave cloth. Some done the spinnin', and there was more of 'em to do the sewin'. Miss Ellen, she looked after all that and cut out most of the clothes. She saw that us had plenty to wear. Sometimes Marster would go to the sewin' house, and Mist'ess would tell him to get on away from there and look after his own work, that her and Aunt Julia could run that loom house. Marster, he just laughed then and told us chillun what was hangin' round the door to just listen to them women cackle.

Us had water buckets, called piggins, what was made out of cedar and had handles on the sides. Sometimes us sawed off little vinegar kegs and put handles on 'em. Us loved to drink out of gourds. There was lots of gourds raised every year. Some of 'em was so big they was used to keep eggs in, and for lots of things us use baskets for now. Them little gourds made fine dippers.

Them corn shuckin's was sure big-enough times. When us got all the corn gathered up and put in great, long piles, then the gettin' ready was started. Why, them women cooked for days, and the men would get the shoats ready to barbecue. Marster would send us out to get the slaves from the farms round about there.

The place was all lit up with lightwood-knot torches

and bonfires, and there was excitement a-plent when all the niggers got to singin' and shoutin' as they made the shuck fly. One of them songs went something like this:

> "Oh! my head, my poor head,
> Oh! my poor head is 'fected."

There weren't nothin' wrong with our heads—that was just our way of lettin' our overseer know us wanted some liquor. Pretty soon, he would come round with a big horn of whiskey, and that made the poor head well, but it wasn't long 'fore it got worse again, and then us got another horn of whiskey. When the corn was all shucked, then us ate all us could, and let me tell you, that was some good eatin'. Then us danced the rest of the night.

Next day when us all felt so tired and bad, Marster would tell us 'bout stayin' up all night, but Mist'ess took up for us, and that tickled old Marster. He just laughed and said, "Will you listen to that woman?" Then he would make some of us sing one of them songs us had done been singin' to dance by. It goes sort of like this:

> "Turn your partner round!
> Steal round the corner,
> 'Cause them Johnson gals is hard to beat!
> Just glance round and have a good time!
> Them gals is hard to find!"

That's just 'bout all I can recollect of it now.

The big war was 'bout over when them Yankees come by our place and just went through everything. They called all the slaves together and told 'em they was free and didn't belong to nobody no more, and said the slaves could take all they wanted from the smokehouses and barns and the big house, and could go when and where they wanted to go. They tried to hand us out all the meat and hams, but us told 'em us weren't hungry, 'cause Marster had always done give us all us wanted. When they couldn't make none of us take nothin', they said it was the strangest thing they had done ever seen, and that that man Echols must have sure been good to his niggers.

When them Yankees had done gone off, Marster come out to our place. He blowed the bugle to call us all up to the house. He couldn't hardly talk, 'cause somebody told him that them Yankees couldn't talk his niggers into stealin' nothin'. Marster said he never knowed 'fore how good us loved him. He told us he had done tried to be good to us and had done the best he could for us and that he was might proud of the way every one of us had done behaved ourselves. He said that the war was over now, and us was free and could go anywhere us wanted to, but that us didn't have to go if us wanted to stay there. He said he would pay us for our work and take care of us if us stayed, or if us wanted to work on shares he would 'low us to work some land that way. A few of them niggers drifted off, but most of 'em stayed right there 'til they died.

Me, I stayed right on there 'til after Marster died. He was sick a long, long time, and one morning old Mist'ess, she called to me. "Robert," she said, "you ain't going to have no Marster long, 'cause he's 'bout gone." I called all the niggers up to the big house, and when they was in the yard, Mist'ess, she said, "Robert, you been with us so long, you can come in and see him 'fore he's gone for good." When I got in that room, I knowed the Lord had done laid His hand on my good old marster, and he was a-goin' to that home he used to preach to us niggers 'bout, and it 'peared to me like my heart would just bust. When the last breath was done gone, I went back in the yard and told the other niggers, and there was sure cryin' and prayin' 'mongst 'em, 'cause all of 'em loved Marster.

That was sure one big funeral. Mist'ess said she wanted all of Marster's old slaves to go, 'cause he loved 'em so, and all of us went. Some what had done been gone for years come back for Marster's funeral.

Next day, after the funeral was over, Mist'ess, she said, "Robert, I want you to stay on with me 'cause you know how he wanted his work done." Then Mist'ess' daughter and her husband, Mr. Dickenson, come there to stay. None of us niggers liked that Mr. Dickenson, and most of 'em left, and then 'bout two years after Marster died Mist'ess went to Atlanta to stay with another of her daughters, and she died there. When Mist'ess left, I left, too, and come on here to Athens, and I been here ever since.

Elsie Moreland

*Age 85 when interviewed
at her home
in Hawkinsville, Georgia*

I DON'T EVEN REMEMBER my mother. She died when I was too little to remember. But I heard folks say that she come from Virginny and was sold to our marster in Houston County. That's where me and my sister was born. My mother had some more chillun where she come from but left 'em up there, and I never did know 'em. I was the youngest child.

My daddy's name was Jack Moreland. My daddy was a carpenter. Marster hired him out to other folks. Sometimes he'd even go way down to Savannah, so I never saw him much. I'd stay round at nights in other nigger cabins, and Granny'd look after me in the daytime. Granny'd keep all the little nigger chillun every day, while they folks worked in the fields.

I was a little gal, 'bout six or eight years old, when they put me to sweeping yards. Then I'd drive the cows to the pasture. When I got bigger, I toted water to the field hands, and when they was ginnin' cotton I drove the gin with four mules hitched to it. My sister, she was a waitress in the white [plantation] house.

I remember when I was real little, I'd set right at my marster's feet, and he'd feed me. He whipped me when I got to mischief, but I needed it. All chillun do. He had overseers on the place to whip the grown niggers if they was bad, but old Miss wouldn't let 'em touch us little ones. Her marster'd 'tend to us. They was kind and good to everybody. I got along a lot better than I do now. They never mistreated nobody.

The slaves had a lot of what they called frolics. When they got through working at night, they'd all meet in one of their cabins and dance and pat and sing. Course, I was little, but I 'member something about it. Lots of time, the white folks give 'em something good to eat after they'd danced. Sometimes the slaves'd have corn shuckings. We had a big day on the Fourth of July. The white folks give us a big dinner spread on long tables in their backyard. We'd sure have something good to eat—chicken, turkey, barbecue, cakes, and pies. Then we'd dance and play games after dinner. At Christmastime, the marster'd always give us presents. I 'member he'd give the women and girls new dresses and the men and boys new suits.

Marster was a Methodist, so that's where we went. We never lived far from the church, so we'd all walk. There was a place back of the white folks where we sat.

That was the only place a slave could go without a pass. They never give me no pass; they made me stay in the yard. But the grown ones would have to have a pass if they wanted to visit. The patterollers sure would get 'em if they caught 'em without a pass. The niggers'd do some fast running to get away from them patterollers, 'cause if they got home Marster wouldn't let 'em be touched.

I never did no courting then. I was too little, but I 'member about my sister. She had two fellas coming to see her, and I know they brung her candy 'cause I got some of it. She never had no preacher to marry her; she and the man just lived together, 'cause that's the way they done in them days. It was a long time after Freedom before I married.

I remember one time when I was sick. Old Miss give me some lobelia. It sure was bitter, but I had to take it 'cause it kept off the fever.

Rations was given out every Monday night. They was 'sposed to last a week, but some of them'd eat 'em up quick and go back and get some more. There was always plenty to eat, so they could get it most anytime. Granny fed us little niggers. On fair days, she'd take the dinner trays out in the yard, and we'd eat under the trees. But there was a regular room for us to eat in if it rained. We had greens, peas, meat, bread, and plenty of milk all the time. On Sundays, they give us biscuit, chicken, and cake. It was enough for anybody. Everything we ate was raised on the farm except sugar and coffee. The niggers could go hunting and fishing right there on the place any night they wanted to.

There was some nigger woman on the place that'd weave the cloth and make the clothes. There was a house for the weaving and one where clothes was made. Old Miss looked after it. But they never fit no clothes on us, 'cause there was too many. They'd make a dress for me and tell me to get.

The marster freed us after the war. But we-all stay with him 'til after Christmas. Then some of the niggers moved away, and some rented land from him and stayed right there. Me and my daddy stayed with him about a year after Freedom, and then my daddy got work somewhere else, and I had to go with him.

I DON'T KNOW how old I is. George [her husband] is nigh 'bout ninety. I remembers all 'bout them Yankees. How come I remember 'bout them, and the war was over then? I can't tell you that, but I knows I remember seein' 'em in the big road. It might not have been Mr. Sherman's men, but Mammy said the Yankees was in the big road long after Freedom was declared, and they was down here getting things straight. They was sure in a mess after the war! Everythin' was tore up, and the poor niggers didn't know which way to turn.

My mammy's name was Catherine Bass, and my

pappy was Ephriam Butts. Us belonged to Marse Ben Bass, and my mammy had the same name as Marster until she married Pappy. He belonged to somebody else 'til Marster bought him. They had ten chillun. Mammy didn't have no doctor. Didn't nobody hardly have a doctor in them days. The white folks used yarbs [herbs] and old women to help them at that time. Mammy had a old woman who lived on the place every time she had a little one. She had one every year, too. She lost one. That chile run aroun' 'til she was one year old and then died with the dysentery.

Us had a right hard time in them days. The beds us used then weren't like these here nice beds us has nowadays. Us worked in the old days from before sunup 'til black night, and us knowed what work was. The beds us slept on had round posts made outen saplin's of hickory or little pine trees. The bark was took off, and they was rubbed slick and shiny. The springs was rope crossed from one side of the bed to the other. The mattress was straw or cotton in big sacks made outen osnaburg or big salt sacks pieced together.

Mammy didn't have much soap, and she used to scrub the floor with sand, and it was just as white. She made all the soap us used, but it took a heap.

We cooked in the ashes and on hot coals, but the vittles tasted a heap better than they does nowadays. Mammy had to work in the field and then come home and cook for Marster and his family. I didn't know nothing 'bout it 'til after Freedom, but I heard 'em tell 'bout it.

Mammy and Pappy stayed on Marster's plantation 'til a year or more after they had they Freedom. Marster paid 'em wages and a house to stay in. He didn't have many slaves—'bout twenty, I reckon. My brothers was Berry, Daniel, Ephriam, Tully, Bob, Lin, and George. The others I disremembers 'cause they left home when they was big enough to earn they livin', and I just don't recollect.

Conjure woman! I aims to get to Heaven when I dies, and I sure don't know how to conjure nobody. I ain't never seen no ghost. I always pray to the Lord that He spare me that trouble and not let me see nary one. No good in folks plunderin' on this earth after they leave here the first time.

If my mammy or pappy ever runned away from Marster, I ain't heard tell of it, but Mammy said that when slaves did run away they was caught and whipped by the overseer. If a man or a woman killed another one, then they was branded with a hot iron. A big **S** was put on they face somewheres. **S** stood for slave, and everybody knowed they was a murderer. Master didn't have no overseer; he overseed hisself.

Why is George so white? 'Cause his marster was a white gentleman named Mr. Jimmie Dunn. His mammy was a colored woman named Frances Mason, and his marster was his paw. That happened a lot in them days. I heard tell of a white man what would tell his sons to go down to them nigger quarters and "get me more slaves." He [George's master] made George his overseer as soon as he was big enough to boss the other slaves.

I ain't had no education. I 'tended school part of one term, but I was so scared of my teacher that I couldn't learn nothing. He was an old white man. He had been teaching for years and years, but he had cancer, and they had done stopped him from teaching white chillun. His name was Mr. Bill Breer. I was scared 'cause he was a white man. No white man ain't never harmed me, but I was scared of him anyhow. One day, he says to me, "Chile, I ain't going to hurt you none 'cause I'm white." He was mighty good old man. He would have learned us more, but he died the next year. Mammy paid him ten cents a month apiece for all us chillun. The boys would work for they money, but I was the onliest gal, and Mammy wouldn't let me go off the plantation to make none. What I made there, I got, but I didn't make much 'til after I married.

Does you want to know 'bout my marriage? Well, I was fifteen years old, and I had a preacher to marry me. His name was Andrew Brown. In them days, us always waited 'til the time of year when us had a big meeting or at Christmastime. Then if one of us wanted to get married, he would perform the wedding after the meeting or after Christmas celebratin'. I had [a] bluish worsted dress. I married in January, right after Christmas. At my marriage, us had barbecue, Brunswick stew, and cake. The whole yard was full of folks.

Mammy was a religious woman, and the first day of

Christmas she always fasted half a day, and then she would pray. After that, everybody would have eggnog and barbecue and cake, if they had the money to buy it. Mammy said that when they was still slaves, Marster always gived 'em Christmas, but after they had Freedom then they had to buy they own rations. Us would have banjo playing and dance the Pije-Wing and the Shuffle-Toe.

George's pa didn't leave him no land when he died. Us went to another farm and rented when the marriage was over. George's pa wasn't dead, but he didn't offer to do nothing for us.

I had eight chillun of my own. Us ain't never had no land us could call ours. Us just moved from one farm to another all our days. This here land us is on now belongs to Mr. Cline. My son and his chillun works it, and they give us what they can spare. The Red Cross lady helps us get along somehow or another.

James Bolton
Age 85 when interviewed

MY PAW, HE WAS named Whitfield Bolton, and Liza Bolton was my maw. Charlie, Edmund, Thomas, and John Bolton was my brothers, and I had one sister; she was Rosa. We belonged to Marse Whitfield Bolton, and we lived on his plantation in Oglethorpe County near Lexington, not far from the Wilkes County line.

We stayed in a one-room log cabin with a dirt floor. A frame made out of pine poles was fastened to the wall, to hold up the mattresses. Our mattresses was made out of cotton baggin' stuffed with wheat straw. Our covers was quilts made out of old clothes. Slave women too old to work in the fields made the quilts.

Maw, she went up to the big house once a week to

get the 'lowance of vittles. They 'lowanced us a week's rations at a time. It was generally hog meat, cornmeal, and sometimes a little flour. Maw, she done our cooking on the coals in the fireplace at our cabin.

We had plenty of possums and rabbits and fishes, and sometimes we had wild turkeys and partridges. Slaves won't supposed to go huntin' at night, and everybody know you can't catch no possums 'cept at night. Just the same, we had plenty possums, and nobody ask how we caught 'em.

Now 'bout them rabbits! Slaves won't 'lowed to have no guns and no dogs of they own. All the dogs on our plantation belonged to my employer—I means, to my marster—and he 'lowed us to use his dogs to run down the rabbits. Nigger mens and boys would go in crowds—sometimes as many as twelve at one time—and a rabbit ain't got no chance 'gainst a lot of niggers and dogs, when they light out for to run him down.

What wild critters we wanted to eat and couldn't run down, we was right smart 'bout catchin' in traps. We caught lots of wild turkeys and partridges in traps and nets.

Long Crick runned through our plantation, and the river weren't no far piece off. We sho' did catch the fishes—mostly cats and perch and heaps and heaps of suckers. We caught our fishes most generally with hook and line, but the carpenters on our plantation knowed how to make basket traps that sho' enough did lay in the fishes. God only knows how long it has been since this old nigger pulled a big shad out of the river. Ain't no shads been caught in the river round here in so long I don't remember when.

We didn't have no gardens of our own round our cabins. My employer—I means, my marster—had one big garden for our whole plantation, and all his niggers had to work in it whenever he wanted 'em to. Then he give 'em all plenty good garden just for themselves. They was collards and cabbage and turnips and beets and English peas and beans and onions, and they was always some garlic for ailments. Garlic was mostly to cure worms. They roasted the garlic in the hot ashes and squeeze the juice out of it and made the chillun take it. Sometimes they made poultices out of garlic for the pneumony.

We saved a heap of bark from wild cherry and poplar and black haw and slippery elm trees, and we dried out mullein leaves. They was all mixed and brewed to make bitters. Whenever a nigger got sick, them bitters was good for, well, they was good for what ailed 'em. We took 'em for rheumatiz, for fever, and for the misery in the stomach, and for 'most all sorts of sickness. Red oak bark tea was good for sore throat.

I never seen no store-bought clothes 'til long after Freedom done come. One slave woman done all the weavin' in a separate room called the loom house. The cloth was dyed with homemade colorin'. They used indigo for blue, red oak bark for brown, green husks off of warnicks [black walnut trees] for black, and sumacs for red, and they would mix these colors to make other colors. During the summertime, we just wore shorts and pants made out of plain cotton cloth. They wove some wool in with the cotton to make the cloth for our winter clothes. The wool was raised right there on our plantation. We had our own shoemaker man. He was a slave named Buck Bolton, and he made all the shoes the niggers on our plantation wore.

When slaves got married, they just laid down the broom on the floor, and the couple joined hands and jumped backwards over the broomstick. I done seen 'em married that way many a time. Sometimes my marster would fetch Mist'ess down to the slave quarters to see a weddin'. If the slaves gettin' married was house servants, sometimes they married on the back porch or in the backyard at the big house, but plantation niggers what was field hands married in they own cabins. The bride and groom just wore plain clothes, 'cause they didn't have no more. Folkses didn't make no big to-do over weddings like they do now.

When the young marsters and mist'esses at the big houses got married, they 'lowed the slaves to gather on the porch and peep through the windows at the wedding. Most generally, they would give the young couple a slave or two to take with them to they new home. My marster's chillun was too young to get married before the war was over. They was seven of them chillun—four was gals and the rest was boys.

My employer—I means, my marster and my mist'ess—they was sho' all-right white folkses. I don't know much 'bout the big house, 'cause I was a plantation nigger and I weren't no house servant. I remember they lived in the big house. It was all painted brown. I heard tell there was more than nine hundred acres in our plantation, and lots of folkses lived on it. The biggest portion was woods.

We had one overseer at a time, and he always lived at the big house. The overseers weren't quality white folkses like our marster and mist'ess, but we never heard nothing 'bout no poor white trash in them days, and if we heard somethin' like that we would have knowed better than to let Marster hear us make such talk. Marster made us call his overseer "Mister." We had one overseer named Mr. Andrew Smith, and another time we had a overseer named Mr. Pope Short. Overseers was just there on the business of getting the work done. They saw after everybody doing his work accordin' to order.

My employer—I mean, my marster—never 'lowed no overseer to whip none of his niggers. Marster done all the whippin' on our plantation hisself. He never did make no big bruises, and he never drawed no blood, but he sho' could burn 'em up with that lash. Niggers on our plantation was whipped for laziness mostly. Next to that, whippin's was for stealin' eggs and chickens. They fed us good and plenty, but a nigger is just bound to pick up chickens and eggs if he can, no matter how much he done eat. He just can't help it. If a nigger ain't busy, he going to get into mischief.

I weren't nothin' but a chile when Freedom come. And in slavery time, chillun won't 'lowed to do no work, 'cause the marsters wanted their niggers to grow up big and strong and didn't want 'em stunted none. That's how come I didn't get no more beatin's than I did. My employer—I means, my marster—never give me but one lickin'. He had done told me to watch the cows and keep 'em in the pasture. I caught lots of grasshoppers and started fishing in the crick runnin' through the pasture, and first thing I knows the overseer was roundin' up all the other niggers to get the cows out of the cornfield. I knows then my time is done come.

Now and then, slaves would run away and go in the woods and dig dens and live in them. Sometimes they runned away on account of cruel treatment, but most of the time they runned away 'cause they just didn't want to work and want to laze around for a spell. The marsters always put the dogs after 'em and get 'em back. They had black-and-brown dogs called "nigger hounds" what weren't used for nothin' but to track down niggers.

There weren't no such place as a jail where we was. If a nigger done somethin' disorderly, they just naturally took a lash to him. I ain't never seen no nigger in chains 'til long after Freedom done come, when I seen 'em on the chain gangs.

The overseer woke us up at sunrise—lessen they called it sunrise. We would finish our vittles and be in the fields ready for work before us see no sun. We laid off of work at sunset, and they didn't drive us hard. Leastwise, they didn't on our plantation. I done heard they was mighty hard on 'em on other plantations.

My marster never did 'low his niggers worked after sundown.

I never knowed Marster to sell but one slave, and he just had bought her from the market at New Orleans. She say it lonesome off on the plantation and asked the marster to sell her to folks living in town. After he done sold her, every time he go to town, she begged him to buy her back, but he didn't pay her no more attention. When they had sales of slaves on the plantations, they let everybody know what time the sale going to be. When the crowd get together, they put the niggers on the block and sell 'em. Leastwise, they call it "puttin' 'em on the block." They just fetch 'em out and show 'em and sell 'em.

There weren't no church for niggers on our plantation, and we went to the white folks' church and listened to the white preachers. We sat behind a partition. Sometimes on a plantation, a nigger claim he done been called to preach, and if he can get his marster's consent he can preach round under trees and in cabins when it ain't work time. These nigger preachers in slavery time was called "cheerbackers." There weren't no cheerbackers 'lowed to baptize none of Marster's niggers. White preachers done our baptizin' in Long Crick. When we went to be baptized, they always sung "Amazin' Grace, How Sweet the Sound."

When folks on our plantation died, Marster always let many of us as wanted to go lay off of work 'til after the burying. Sometimes it were two or three months after the burying before the funeral sermon was preached. Right now, I can't recollect no song we sung at funerals except "Hark, from the Tombs a Doleful Sound."

None of our niggers ever runned away, and we didn't know nothin' 'bout no North 'til long after Freedom done come. We visited round each other's cabins at night. I did hear tell 'bout the patterollers. Folkses said that if they caught niggers out at night, they would give 'em "what Paddy give the drum."

After supper, we used to gather round and knock tin buckets and pans. We beat 'em like drums. Some use their fingers and some use sticks for to make the drum sounds, and 'most always somebody blowed on quills. Quills was a row of whistles made out of reeds, or sometimes they made 'em out of bark. Every whistle in the row was a different tone, and you could play any kind of tune you wants if you had a good row of quills. They sho' did sound sweet.

Spring plowin' and hoein' times, we worked all day Saturdays, but most generally we laid off of work at twelve o'clock Saturday. That was dinnertime. Saturday nights, we played and danced, sometimes in the cabins and sometimes in the yards. If we didn't have a big stack of fat kindling wood lit up to dance by, sometimes the mens and womans would carry torches of kindling wood while they danced, and it sho' was a sight to see. We danced the Turkey Trot and Buzzard Lope, and how we did love to dance the Mary Jane! We would get in a ring, and when the music started we would begin workin' our feet while we sung "You Steal My True Love, and I Steal You'ens."

We never did no work on Sundays on our plantation. The church was 'bout nine miles from the plantation, and we all walked there. Anybody too old and feeble to walk the nine miles just stayed home, 'cause Marster didn't 'low his mules used none on Sunday. All 'long the way, niggers from other plantations would join us, and sometimes befo' we get to the church house they would be forty or fifty slaves comin' along the road in a crowd. Preaching generally lasted 'til 'bout three o'clock. In summertime, we had dinner on the ground at the church. We didn't have no barbecue like they does now. Everybody cooked 'nough on Saturday and fetched it in baskets.

Christmas, we always had plenty good to eat, and we all got together and had lots of fun. We ran up to the big house early Christmas mornin' and holler out, "Mornin', Christmas gift!" Then they give us plenty of Sandy Claus, and we'd go back to our cabins to have fun 'til New Year's Day. We knowed Christmas was over and gone when New Year's Day come, 'cause we got back to work that day, after frolickin' all Christmas week.

We would sing and pray Easter Sunday, and on Easter Monday we frolicked and danced all day long.

'Bout the most fun we had was at corn shuckin's, where they put the corn in long piles and call in the folks from the plantations nigh round to shuck it. Sometimes four or five hundred head of niggers would be shuckin' corn at one time. When the corn all done been shucked, they'd drink the liquor the marsters give 'em and then frolic and dance from sundown to sunup. We started shuckin' corn 'bout dinnertime and tried to finish by sundown, so we could have the whole night for frolic. Some years, we would go to ten or twelve corn shuckin's in one year.

I ain't never forgotten when Mist'ess died. She had been so good to every nigger on our plantation. When we got sick, Mist'ess always had us tended to. The niggers on our plantation all walked to church to hear her funeral sermon and then walked to the graveyard to the buryin'. It never was the same on our plantation after we done laid Mist'ess away.

We didn't know nothin' 'bout games to play. We played with the white folks' chillun and watched after 'em, but most of the time we played in the crick what runned through the pasture. Nigger chillun was always scared to go in the woods after dark. Folks done told us Raw Head and Bloody Bones live in the woods and get little chillun and eat 'em up if they got out in the woods after dark.

"Rock-Bye Baby, in the Treetops" was the only song I heard my maw sing to get her babies to sleep. Slave folks sung 'most all the time, but we didn't think of what we sung much. We just got happy and started singing. Sometimes we would sing if we felt sad and low-down, but soon as we could we would go off where we could go to sleep and forget all 'bout troubles. When you hear a nigger singin' sad songs, it's just 'cause he can't stop what he is doin' long enough to go to sleep.

My employer—I means, my marster—didn't have no bell. He has 'em blow bugles to wake up his hands and to call 'em from the fields. Sometimes the overseer blowed the bugle. If nobody else was at the house, the cook blowed it. Mist'ess done learned the cook to count the clock. None of the rest of our niggers could count the clock.

One morning, Marster blowed the bugle his own self and called us all up to the big house yard. He told us, "You-all just as free as I is. You are free from under the taskmaster but ain't free from labor. You got to labor and work hard if you aim to live and eat and have clothes to wear. You can stay here and work for me, or you can go wherever you please." He said he would pay us what was right, and it's the truth didn't nary a nigger on our plantation leave our marster then.

I worked on with Marster for forty years after the war. Right soon after the war, we saw plenty of Ku Kluxers, but they never bothered nobody on our plantation. They always seemed to be havin' heaps of fun. Course, they did have to straighten out some of them brash young nigger bucks on some of the other farms round 'bout. Most of the niggers the Ku Kluxers got after weren't on no farm, but was just roamin' round talkin' too much and makin' trouble. They had to take 'em in hand two or three time befo' some of them fool free niggers could be learned to behave themselves. But them Ku Kluxers kept on after 'em 'til they learned they just got to be good if they expects to stay round here.

Just befo' Freedom comed, 'bout fifty Yankee soldiers come through our plantation and told us that the bullwhips and cowhide was all dead and buried. Them soldiers just passed on in a hurry and didn't stop for a meal of vittles or nothin'.

We didn't talk much 'bout Mr. Abraham Lincoln durin' slavery time, 'cause we was scared of him after the war got started. I don't know nothin' 'bout Mr. Jefferson Davis; I don't remember ever hearin' 'bout him. I heard 'bout Mr. Booker Washington, and they do say he runned a mighty good school for niggers.

It was 'bout forty years after the war befo' many niggers begun to own their own land. They didn't know nothin' 'bout tendin' to money business when the war done ended, and it took 'em a long time to learn how to buy and sell and take care of what they make. And heaps of niggers ain't never learned nothin' 'bout them things yet.

A long time after the war, I married Liza Yerby. I didn't give Liza no chance for to dress up—just went and took her right out of the white folks' kitchen and married her at the church in her workin' clothes. We had thirteen chillun, but they ain't but two of 'em livin' now. Most of our chillun died babies. Durin' slavery, Mist'ess took care of all the nigger babies borned on our plantations and looked after they mammies, too, but after Freedom come, heap of nigger babies died out.

Both my wives was widows. I married my second

wife thirty-seven years ago. To tell the truth, I don't rightly know how many grandchillun I got, 'cause I ain't seen some of 'em for thirty years. My chillun is off from here, and I don't know to save my life where they is or what they do. My sister and brothers, they is dead, what ain't gone off, and I don't know for sure where none of 'em is now.

I was thirty years old when I joined the church. Nobody ought to join no church 'til he is truly born of God, and if he is truly born of God he going to know it. If you want a restin' place after you leave this old world, you ought to get ready for it now.

Now I'm going to tell you the truth. Now that it's all over, I don't find life so good in my old age as it was in slavery, when I was chillun down on Marster's plantation. Then I didn't have to worry 'bout where my clothes and my somethin' to eat was comin' from, or where I was going to sleep. Marster took care of all that. Now I ain't able to work and make a living, and it's sho' mighty hard on this old nigger.

Cora Shepherd
Age 82 when interviewed
in Beech Island, South Carolina

I AM EIGHTY-TWO years going on eighty-three this month and can't hardly see, so I sits here and nurse the baby. Sometimes I look off yonder and try to see into Columbia County again.

I belonged to Jesse Walden up in Columbia County from the time I was born until the finish. My mother was the house woman—washer and ironer and weaver. My father was the hog minder and marked cattle. I just played about in the fields 'til I got big enough to go in the house and fan flies when they was eating. Old Marster wouldn't let his little niggers work out and get sunstroke.

Us little chaps didn't do no work. They give us

things to 'muse us, like. Us get bark for the mammy—she was the nurse that tend the little chaps and made 'em call her Mammy. Us played in the orchards, picked up rotten fruit, cleaned up like that. They put the bigger children out in the fields pickin' peas. "You take that one," they said, "and train him how to pick peas." But you couldn't stay in the fields no later than nine o'clock, 'count of the sun. Then at four or five in the afternoon, we had to get up our bark to cook on.

Once, us little chaps pulled a lot of green apples. Some of 'em had salt. Old Miss was watching us from the porch. She sent the house woman to tell us all to come up; she wanted to give us a lecture. She give us five licks apiece, the onliest licks I ever got. Miss say she wanted us to learn better.

All the children what had mothers in the house, my old miss would give 'em meals from the kitchen. Every morning, us had to go to the kitchen, and they give us milk, meat, and bread. At twelve o'clock—there was over a hundred head of little darkies—us would go out and get bark for 'em to cook with. The old lady—Mammy, the one what nurse the little niggers—she had a wash pot full of peas for us little darkies. My old marster fed his niggers, I tell you the truth about him. Then at four o'clock every afternoon, us had milk, and us got night bread.

My marster had seven big plantations from Columbia County to Petersburg Road and then down to Georgia Road. He set right in the fork of the road above Dr. Phinizy's old place.

My old marster didn't let his niggers be whipped. He had a settlement overseer once, and he turned him off. I remember when he turned off Mr. Shanklin. My old marster went to his Wrightsboro plantation every Friday. He give his niggers 'lowance on Saturday afternoon and knock 'em all off. Well, Mr. Shanklin wouldn't give 'em anything to eat, and four men, they went and killed a beef and tore it up because they hadn't had a mouthful, and give all the people on the place some. When the overseer hear about it, he whipped them four men.

Marster comes back on Monday at one o'clock. We loved him, and when we see him comin' up the road us run and catch his coattails, then he would carry us to the barn and give us all a couple of shorts [tiny gifts]. Marster come down to the quarters and call all the little niggers around him. He sat down under a great big shade tree, and we was all so glad to see him. The mammy what nurse the little darkies say, "Marster, we had a big whipping since you been gone." Marster said, "Yes. Your missus tell me." Then Mammy said, "We was all hungry." Marster got up. "That won't be the case no more," and he started off. He call that overseer and give him a wagon and team to move his things with and run him right off the place! You see, I had a good marster, but some of the old marsters weren't so good. Marster never did have no bands [of patterollers] or nothin' like that on his place.

When niggers marry, white boss marry 'em. He

would go to the courthouse and get a commit from the head man and come back. They just go up to the house, and he marry 'em, give you a house, and you start living together. My old marster didn't have but one man on his place that had a family off of it.

Us went to white folks' church, sat in the back, and it was the beautifulest place! The water down the hill just spewin' out! It was called Greenbrier Church, near Cedar Rock.

My old marster let us have prayer meeting Saturday night regular. Colored man preach. Better not disturb his niggers when old carriage driver John Jefferson preach! I 'member his text—"Love yo' marster. Love yo' miss. Obey! Be subdued to yo' marster and yo' miss." Then he would preach, "Marvel not—ye must be born again!"

We used to hide under a fig bush when the patterollers come by, riding down the road tootin' and hollerin'. Once, they caught one of my old marster's niggers without the strip what say, "This is a Walden darky. Let him pass." They whipped the man when he went to his wife. He said, "Marster, one of my children was sick, and I wouldn't worry you for a strip before Wednesday night, so I tried to slip down there." Marster told him, "Why, I would have told 'em not to whip you. Don't do that no more."

My old miss sent the little ones in the field. We got wheat and oat straw to make mats for the soldiers in the army. My old miss have clothes made and send to the army for soldiers, too. There was two seamsters in the house cuttin' and sewin' every day for the hands and the soldiers.

Marster said when we hear them [Confederate soldiers returning from the war], us go in the woods and hide, 'cause he didn't know what they might do to the little chaps. We could see them ride up there with they tin cans and blankets hung on the skinny horses. Some be so hungry they get off the old horse and go round in the lot and bust open the barn door and throw the corn everywhere. They went to old Miss and ask her for the key, and she give it to 'em, and they got hams and shoulders out the smokehouse and cut off the fat and eat the lean. They was worse than the Yankees. Some had the 'dacity to go to the house and search for clothes!

[After the war, Cora's master was taken ill.] He call us all in the room. Sent the house woman, Anne, to call us. He lay there lookin' at us. "All my little darkies," he said, and I will never forget that—us all standing round looking at him so sick. "I hate to see you all scattered, but as long as you live I want you to stay here, and when you buried I want you buried on the Walden premises." The darkies hollered, "Us don't want you to die, Marster. Us won't get no mo' shorts!" They didn't know no better, you see. Marster bust out in a cry, and all us children bellowed, too. "I am born to die," he told us, and after that he die. He told my old miss to tell us every one as we growed up our age every year, and whilst she was livin' she did. I stayed right there 'til I got grown and married right out of my miss's house. I slept every night in her room—pull out my little trundle bed and shove it back in the morning.

My old miss didn't allow nobody disturbin' her place, 'cause she was a widow. They [the Ku Klux Klan] catch people and kill 'em and lynch 'em. I seen four men they killed thataway! Caught 'em and beat 'em to death, but I ain't never know what for. They rode horses and had great big sheets wrapped around 'em.

Nights, I would be settin' in the room with my old miss, and she knittin'. She would try to give my lessons. She cut doll clothes for me to sew and give me pictures out of papers to cut. I stayed in they house fifteen years after I married. After my old miss dies, the boys was all married. They give every one a plantation. Then Mr. Jim Lamkin married Miss Ella, and she got possession of the home. Then all the colored people left.

The last time I went up home—I calls it my home 'cause it is my home—after Marster die, I went from Beech Island to see old Miss. I stayed a week and didn't eat two meals in colored persons' houses. She wouldn't allow us to eat out. She said, "Come right up to my house and see me and take yo' meals."

MY MOTHER'S NAME was Violet Mobley, and my father's name was Robert Hammock. They were born in Crawford County, and that's where I was born, too. My marster's name was Henry Mobley, and he was a mighty good man. There was eleven chillun in our family, and I was the seventh child. I'll be ninety-two the sixteenth day of next June.

My marster was the best there was. He had plenty money, too; he wasn't no poor white trash. I reckon there was about five hundred of us niggers. He lived in a big two-story white house, and he and old Miss and their three chillun was all the time having company. Marster believed in sending his chillun to school, too. We lived three miles from Knoxville, Georgia, so that's where they went to school.

We lived about thirty miles from Macon, so the crops was carried there. We raised lots of cotton, corn, and pumpkins. My brother John, he was the wagoner and drove six horses. The other drivers 'most always drove two horses. It would take a day to go to Macon and a day to come back. They'd camp a few miles from Macon for the night.

My father worked in the field. Most of my brothers and sisters worked there, too. My mother was the marster's cook. She did all the cookin' for the white folks and the niggers, too. Course, she had a helper, but she had a lots of work to do anyhow. She'd cook for the slaves in a great big wash pots.

The first work I 'member doing was helping clean the house. I was about twelve or fourteen then. Going to Knoxville for the mail was another of my jobs. I'd ride a pony and had a big bag for the mail. On school days, I drove the girls into town to school. They rode in a phaeton, and the driver's seat was built over the other seats. The girls could keep nice and warm in the phaeton.

I slept in a little trundle bed right in the room with Marster and Mist'ess. Then if they needed anything, I'd be right there to get it. And I didn't want for nothing. I'd think I was white 'til I looked in the glass. Whenever I wanted a new suit, I'd just tell my mist'ess, and she'd say, "Well, Bucky, I'll have to see about it." And I'd have a new suit in a day or two.

I reckon my marster was some better to me 'cause I lived right there in the house with them. But he was might good to all of us. Sometimes he had to whip some of the boys, but he never did touch the grown niggers. Whenever they'd disobey, he'd cut off their hair, and that was a bad punishment to them, 'cause they'd try to make their hair grow long. He never did whip me, but I needed it plenty of times.

Oh, we all had a good time. Course, Marster made us work, but we always had plenty time for fun. Lots of nights, we'd have corn shuckin's, and we'd fix up for them just like we was fixing for a wedding. My mother would have all kinds of nice refreshments for us. Then sometimes we'd have a dance. We could invite our friends from other plantations to come sometimes. On Fourth of July, we always had a big barbecue. We had plenty lemonade, custards, pies, cakes, and everything good. On that day, we played all kinds of games, and some of the men would tussle. Sometimes the marster would give us all a little spending money. We didn't have much celebrating at Christmas, but we could go visit our friends.

We went with Marster's family [to church]. Sometimes there'd be two wagonloads full of niggers going to church. We always sat in the back of the church 'cause that was our regular place. Marster let us clear an oak grove on the plantation, and we'd have prayer meetin's there.

I never did go with a lot of girls. Jane, the one I married, lived about a mile from me, so I'd go to see her, and sometimes I'd take candy and handkerchiefs to her. It was after the war when I married, though.

Before the war ever started, I took my young marster to get married. We both dressed up mighty fine, and I drove him over to the lady's house. Young Marster stayed over there that night, and I come back home in the carriage. The next day, we had an affair at our house. We sho' had a good time. Young folks and old folks come from miles around. The tables was in the dining room, and they was just loaded down with good things to eat.

There was a doctor right there on the place, so whenever the slaves were sick he'd look after them. My mother was a kind of a doctor, too. She'd ride horseback all over the place and see how they was getting along. She'd make a tea out of herbs for those who had fever, and sometimes she gave them water from slippery elm.

Most of the slaves would take their food to their cabins. I was right there in the house, so I didn't eat with the other niggers. I ate whatever Marster ate. Course, the slaves had plenty, but we had a little extra. We had something good all the time. Everything we had to eat was raised right there on our plantation 'cept sugar and coffee. Our plantation was rich, and there was always plenty of stuff to eat. Whenever we had time, we'd hunt and fish. Marster even taught me to shoot hisself. He was the best shot I ever saw.

My aunt's job was to weave the cloth. There was a house on the plantation built especially for spinning and weaving. Two or three of the other nigger women made the clothes, and they had to make 'em to fit. The mist'ess would make them be careful so the clothes would look nice. Some of the slaves even learned to dye the wool so that we could have warm clothes in winter. We always had the clothes we needed. Marster wouldn't have us dirty and ragged. It took a lot of cloth for the clothes, too, 'cause everything was made full.

Marster could send corn, lard, and lots of other things to eat to the soldiers. All the food was sent from the plantations to a storehouse and from there to the soldiers. Young Marster went to the war, and his young wife stay with us part the time and with her folks part the time.

One day, a few Yankees came to our plantation and wanted to take our good horses. But we had 'em hid out so they couldn't find 'em. When we really heard the Yankees were coming, we refuged down to Dooly County. Marster bought a place down there, but it wasn't near as fine as the one we left. He carried all his slaves with him, and we worked down there pretty much like we had in Crawford County. But lots of the niggers didn't like Dooly County. The folks was rough down there, and just as soon as the war was over and Marster freed them they went back home to Crawford County. Young Marster came back from the war all right.

I stayed with Marster for a long time [after the war]. Then I worked for another man in the county, but we couldn't get along 'cause I wasn't used to the way he did. I went back to old Marster and stayed 'til I come to Hawkinsville. I was a carpenter 'til I fell off a building, and I ain't never been much good since.

Susan McIntosh
*Age 87 when
interviewed in 1938*

THEY TELL ME I WAS BORN in November 1851, and I know I've been here a long time, 'cause I've seen so many come and go. I've outlived 'most all of my folks 'cept my son that I live with now. Honey, I've 'most forgot about slavery days. I don't read, and anyway there ain't no need to think of them times now.

I was born in Oconee County on Judge William Stroud's plantations. We called him Marse Billy. That was a long time before Athens was the county seat. Ma's name was Mary Jen, and Pa was Christopher Harris. They called him Chris for short. Marster L. G. Harris bought him from Marster Hudson of Elbert County and turned him over to his niece, Miss Lula Harris, when she married Marster Robert Taylor. Marse Robert was a son of a General Taylor that lived in Grady house before it belonged to Mr. Henry Grady's mother. Pa was coachman and houseboy for Miss Lula. Marse Billy owned Ma, and Marse Robert owned Pa, and Pa, he come to see Ma about once or twice a month. The Taylors, they done a heap of travelin' and always took my pa with 'em.

Oh! There was thirteen of us chillun. Seven died soon after they was born, and none of 'em live to get grown 'cept me. Their names was Nanette and Ella, that was next to me; Susan, that's me; Isabelle, Martha, Mary, Diana, Lila, William, Gus, and the twins that was born dead; and Harden. He was named for a Dr. Harden that lived here then.

Marse Billy bought my grandma in Virginia. She was part Injun. I can see her long, straight, black hair now, and when she died she didn't have gray hair like mine. They say Injuns don't turn gray like other folks. Grandma made cloth for the white folks and slaves on the plantation. I used to hand her thread while she was weavin'. The lady that taught Grandma to weave cloth was Mist'ess Gowel, and she was a foreigner, 'cause she wasn't born in Georgia. My aunt Mila Jackson made all the thread that they done the weavin' with.

Grandpa worked for a widow lady that was a seamstress, and she just had a little plantation. She was Mistress Doolittle. All Grandpa done was cut wood, tend the yard and garden. He had rheumatism and couldn't do much.

There ain't much to tell about what we done in the slave quarters, 'cause when we got big enough we had to work—nursin' the babies, totin' water, and helpin' Grandma with the weavin' and such like. Beds was driven to the walls of the cabin, foot- and headboard put together with rails that run from head to foot. Planks was laid crossways and straw put on them, and the bed was covered with the whitest sheets you've ever seen. Some made pallets on the floor.

I didn't make no money 'til after Freedom. I heard tell of ten and fifteen cents, but I didn't know nothing 'bout no figures. I didn't know a nickel from a dime in them days.

Marse Billy 'lowed his slaves to have their own gardens, and 'sides plenty of good garden sass we had milk and butter, bread and meat, chickens, greens, peas, and just everything that growed on the farm. Winter and summer, all the food was cooked in a great big fireplace about four feet wide, and you could put on a whole stick of cordwood at a time. When they wanted plenty of hot ashes to bake with, they burnt wood from ash trees. Sweet potatoes and bread was baked in the ashes. Seems like vittles don't taste as good as they used to, when we cooked like that. Possums, oh! I dearly loved possums. My cousins used to catch 'em, and when they was fixed up and cooked with sweet potatoes possum meat was fit for a king.

Marse Billy had a son named Mark that was a little bitty man. They said he was a dwarf. He never done nothing but play with the children on the plantation.

He would take the children down to the crick that run through the plantation and fish all day.

We had rabbits, but they was most generally caught in a box trap, as there wasn't no time wasted a-huntin' for 'em.

In summer, the slave women wore white homespun and the men wore pants and shirts made out of cloth what looked like overall cloth does now. In winter, we wore the same things, 'cept Marse Billy give the men woolen coats what come down to their knees, and the women wore warm wraps what they called sacks. On Sunday, we had dresses dyed different colors. The dyes were made from red clay and barks. Bark from pine, sweet gums, and blackjacks was boiled, and each one was made a different color dye. The cloth made at home was coarse and was called 'Gusta cloth.

Marse Billy let the slaves raise chickens and cows and have cotton patches, too. They would sell butter, eggs, chickens, brooms made out of wheat straw, and such like. They took the money and bought calico, muslin, and good shoes, pants, coats, and other nice things for their Sunday clothes. Marse Billy bought leather from Marse Brumby's tanyard and had shoes made for us. They was coarse and rough, but they lasted a long time.

My marster was father-in-law of Dr. Jones Long. Marse Billy's wife, Miss Rena, died long before I was born. Their six children was grown when I first knowed 'em. The gals was Miss Rena, Miss Selena, Miss Liza, and Miss Susan. Miss Susan was Dr. Long's wife. I was named for her. There was two boys: Marse John and Marse Mark. I done told you 'bout Marse Mark bein' a dwarf.

They lived in a big old eight-room house on a high hill in sight of Mars Hill Baptist Church. Marse Billy was a great deacon in that church. I heard 'em say that after he had done bought his slaves by working in a blacksmith shop and wearin' cheap clothes like mulberry suspenders, he wasn't goin' to slash his Negroes up. The older folks admired Mistress and spoke well of her. They said she had lots more property than Marse Billy. She said she wanted Marse Billy to see that her slaves was given to her children.

I 'spose there was about a hundred acres on that plantation, and Marse Billy owned more property besides. There was about fifty grown folks, and as to children, I just don't know how many there was. Around the quarters looked like a little town.

Marse Billy had a overseer up to the time war broke out. Then he picked out a reliable colored man to carry out his orders. Sometimes the overseer got rough. Then Marse Billy let him go and got another one. The overseer got us up about four or five o'clock in the morning, and dark brought us in at night.

Jails? I recollect one was in Watkinsville.

I never saw nobody auctioned off, but I heard about it. Men used to come through and buy up slaves for foreign states where there weren't so many.

Well, I didn't have no privilege to learn to read and write, but the white lady that taught my grandma to weave had two sons that run the factory, and they taught my uncles to read and write.

There wasn't no church on the plantation, so we went to the Mars Hill church. The white folks went in the morning from nine 'til twelve, and the slaves went in the evenings from three 'til about five. The white folks went in the front door, and slaves use the back door. Reverend Bedford Lankford that preached to the white folks helped a Negro named Cy Stroud to preach to the Negroes. Oh! I well remember those baptizings. I believe in church and baptizing.

They buried the slaves on the plantation, in coffins made out of pine boards. Didn't put them in two boxes like they do now, and they weren't painted neither.

Marse Bill was good to his slaves, and when they wanted a pass, if it was for a good reason, he give 'em one. Didn't none of Marse Billy's slaves run off to no North. When Marse Billy had need to send news somewhere, he put a reliable Negro on a mule and sent him. I sure didn't hear about no trouble between white folks and Negroes.

When the day's work was over, them slaves went to bed, 'cept when the moon was out and they worked in their own cotton patches. On dark nights, the women mended and quilted sometimes. Not many worked in the fields on Saturday evenings. They caught up on little jobs around the lot, a-mending harness and such like. On Saturday nights, the young folks got together and had little frolics and feasts, but the older folks was getting things ready for Sunday, 'cause Marse Billy was a mighty religious man. We had to go to church, and every last one of the children was dragged along, too.

We always had one week for Christmas. They brought as much of good things to eat as we could destroy in one week, but on New Year's Day we went back to work. As I recollect, we didn't have no corn shuckings or cotton pickings, only what we had to do as part of our regular work.

The white folks mostly got married on Wednesday or Thursday evenin's. Oh! They had fine times, with everything good to eat and lots of dancing, too. Then they took a trip. Some went to Texas and some to Chicago. They call Chicago the colored folks' New York now. I don't remember now weddings 'mongst the slaves. My cousin married on another plantation, but I wasn't there.

Where I was, there wasn't no playing done, only 'mongst the little chillun, and I can't remember much that far back. I recall that we sung a little song about

> "Little drops of water,
> Little drops of sand,
> Make the mighty ocean
> And the pleasant land."

Marse Billy was good to his slaves when they got sick. He called in Dr. Jones Long, Dr. Harden, and Dr. Lumpkin when they was real sick. There was lots of typhoid fever then. I don't know nothing about herbs they used for diseases, only boneset and horehound tea for colds and croup. They put penrile [pennyroyal] in the house to keep out flies and fleas, and if there was a flea in the house we would shoo from that place right then and there.

The old folks put little bags of asafiddy [asafetida] around their chillun's necks to keep off measles and chickenpox, and they used turpentine and castor oil on chillun's gums to make 'em teethe easy. When I was living on Milledge Avenue, I had Dr. Crawford W. Long to see about one of my babies, and he slit that baby's gums so the teeth could come through. That looked might bad to me, but they don't believe in old ways no more.

I don't know nothing about such low-down things as haints and ghosts! Raw Head and Bloody Bones, I just thought he was a skeleton, with no meat on him. Course, lots of Negroes believe in ghosts and haints.

Us chillun done lots of fightin', like chillun will do.

I remember how little Marse Mark Stroud used to take all the little boys on the plantation and teach 'em to play "Dixie" on reeds what they called quills. That was good music, but the radio has done away with all that now.

I knowed I was a slave and that it was the war that set me free. It was about dinnertime when Marse Billy come to the door and called us to the house. He pulled out a paper and read it to us, and then he said, "You are all as free as I am." We couldn't help thinking about what a good marster he always had been, and how old and feeble and gray-headed he looked as he kept a-talkin' that day. "You-all can stay on here with me if you want to," he 'lowed, "but if you do I will have to pay you wages for your work."

*Age 88 when interviewed
in Thomson, Georgia,
on May 18, 1937*

I WAS BORN NEAR the gold mines eighty-eight years ago. And I belonged to Felix Griffin. He didn't have no wife, so Miss Fannie took care of his hands. There was real gold in them mines. Far back as twenty-six years ago, I worked in water and mud up to my waist, drilled many a hole and shot it out with dynamite. Worked at mining fourteen years. Shake it and wash it, and it shine just as pretty! Flux it and retort it, and then they ship it to North Carolina to make into bars.

There wasn't but one thing we suffered for, and that was a brushin' a heap o' times when we needed it! They was good to us. No stealin' amongst our colored folks! If ever was any stealin', we never knowed it.

There was thirty-five or forty people—four families—on the Griffin place where I growed up. There weren't no overseer, 'cause Lonnie, Gabe, Jim, and Felix—the one I belonged to—worked the place theyselves. The big house was white. They had one old man to see after the little chillun like us. Well, we had a quarter with all in there, and the old people made us behave. Didn't do like young folks do now! Good gracious alive! I live out on the Ellington tract. I have seen 'em misbehave—might as well speak to that stone!

But my mother never was no field hand. I learned how to truck cotton after we was set free. She was cook in the big house, her and Grandma. I ate in the house, and I still want my three good meals and a nice driving horse. But I ain't even got a wife now. My first wife was what help me, bless her soul! I learned that after I was free. And I had lovin', good white folks. Yeah, Lonnie got drowned, Jim died, all gone now.

We lived in a heavy log house. At one end was a big chimley. When they had chimley in the middle, two families live in 'em.

My mother and grandmother nurse the little chillun. They mother and fathers hardly know 'em. Mother and Grandma put 'em to bed.

I don't 'member much 'bout prayin'. I went to church in Greenwood Baptist Church, Lincoln County. Well as I can recollect now, Mr. Steed was the pastor. He was a little fellow. They sang spirituals amongst the colored folks, but I never did 'preciate them songs.

I never was drunk, never! I got a different disposition. I don't believe in just any kind o' living.

My father come from Mississippi. My mother was raised up near Raysville. He was sold to the Griffins. You know, they trade you like they trade a horse.

I had plenty something to eat all the time and never was naked for clothes. After I got big enough, I learned to use a loom and used to weave six or seven yards of cloth a day. I wove and reeled some in Thomson, spun there about nine or ten years.

I was a shoemaker, too. Made many a pair of shoes. Old Uncle Jesse Shank taught me to shoe-make.

The masters teach me how to farm and make something of all. Some few people 'lowed to have patches—gardens—too, but there weren't many patches, to my memory.

Mother and Grandma done the cookin' for the whole business. We had big, round bowls as big as a hat full of something to eat, just like a hotel. All the colored folks was fed from the big house.

I used to play banjo, violin, accordion. Last thing I wind up on was the organ, but my organ got burnt up. Wish I had one now to play.

Us had dances, breakdowns, four-hand fatillion [cotillion]. I used to be tip-top; I never did have a person could beat me dancin'. But I never cuss and get drunk and gamble. I got different disposition thataway.

I never did take much stock in haints and signs. I hear folks talkin' 'bout 'em. I weren't superstitious 'bout plantin'; I plant when the ground right.

I used to have plenty around me. After I raise up fourteen chillun, they got at me, wanted to run the business—and they run it in the ground.

I never seed no broomstick wedding. They go before the magister [magistrate] like they was fixin' to got to church. They never put on all these reafs [shows] like they does now.

Each master had a buryin' ground near his place. When niggers died, they bury 'em on the outside. Us all knock off. Make a coffin, put 'em in a wagon, walk in procession to the buryin' ground singing.

I've never suffered for nothing in my life. I tells you, though, God sho' got me in His hands now. I was thirty-one years when I left the Griffin place to make my fortune. Now I ain't got nothing, ain't doin' nothing, don't know where I going to get nothing. Looks like I made a disfortune instead of fortune!

Caroline Ates

*Age 90 when interviewed
in Cochran, Georgia*

My MOTHER'S NAME was Liza Carswell, and I reckon she was born in Montgomery, Alabama, 'cause that's where I was born. I don't known nothing 'bout my daddy, 'cause I never did see him and Mother never did talk to me about him. She had eleven chillun, my mother did, and I was her third child. All her chillun was born durin' slavery times.

Mr. James Carswell was my marster's name, but he died when I was a little girl, so my mother and her family was drawn by his brother, Mr. Bill Carswell. He lived in Wilkinson County and took us there with him to live.

Old Marster was well-to-do. We had three hundred head of niggers. He was a smart man, too, and his chillun all had to go to school. There was always a lot of company at the big house, but my folks never did have many parties.

We lived about thirty-seven miles from Macon, so all the crops was hauled there in great big wagons with six mules to the wagon. We growed lots of cotton, corn, peas, potatoes, rye, and wheat.

My mother did some field work, but most always she cooked for all the slaves that lived near us. She had the nicest kitchen, built especially for that purpose. My brothers and sisters worked in the field.

When I was 'bout eleven, I began toting water to the field hands. Then they started learning me to chop cotton, and I soon began working there, too. I never did no housework 'til after Freedom. One of my aunts cooked for the marster, and another was his housemaid. We had several other maids, too. Marster give one of my sisters to his daughter when she married, and we never see her home 'til we was all free.

Marster was a good man. Sometimes when the niggers didn't do right, he'd have to whip 'em, but he never did mistreat nobody. They was mighty good to me.

At Christmastime, we wouldn't have to work, and we'd have a big dinner up in Marster's backyard—one table for the little niggers and one for the big ones. And we'd have the most to eat! Barbecued chicken, pork, coffee, cakes, and pies. Marster would always give us a dress or something for Christmas. On the Fourth of July, we'd have another big dinner.

Marster was a Baptist. So we went to his church and set in the gallery. Lots of times durin' the week, we'd slip off by ourselves and have prayer meetin'. Then we'd be ready to join the church. I was baptized in the white church. We had to have these meetin's on the plantation 'cause we'd have to get a pass from the marster to leave the place. Sometimes a man would marry a woman that lived on another plantation; Marster would give him a pass twice a week to go to see her. If the niggers were caught without that pass, the patteroller would get 'em.

I was married two years after Freedom. I had quit working in the field and was waiting on old Miss. She had me a bed put right there in her room, and I slept there every night, so if she needed anything I was there to get it. Every night when I'd have company, I'd go talk to him a few minutes, and then I'd go back and stay with old Miss. She give me a big weddin' in the white folks' church, and the white and colored choirs sang. I had on a dress made out of white organdy. After the wedding, we had a feast right in front of Marster's house.

We was well looked after. There was nigger women on the plantation that was sort of nurses, and if anybody got sick they'd tend to 'em. They'd make pepper and dogwood tea for them that had fever. Course, if we got sho'-enough sick, they'd call a doctor. Sometimes even if we was well, we'd have to drink dogwood tea to keep from takin' fever.

Sometimes those that had families wanted to cook in their own cabins, so they was given enough food every Sunday mornin' to last a week. But if it give out, they could get some more. At dinner, we'd most always have greens, peas, meat, potatoes, cornbread, and syrup. But on Sundays, we'd have biscuit. We always had plenty of somethin' to eat. If we ever wanted fish, we could go fishin' right on the place. We could hunt at night, but they wouldn't let the niggers have guns; we'd hunt with dogs.

One of my cousins wove the cloth. She was smart and could weave twelve yards a day. When she'd made her twelve yards, they'd make her get up, 'cause they didn't want her to work too hard. Some of the women made the clothes. They was made full, too, with belts let in at the waist. Sometimes they'd make hoop skirts.

We didn't know much about the war. I 'member, though, one night right before the war, the whole world looked like it was covered with blood. Us niggers didn't know why they was fighting, but every day we'd refugee to the woods, and at night we'd come back. Marster didn't want nothin' to happen to us. The Confederates and Yankee soldiers came to our plantation, but Marster had his best mule and horses and provisions hid in the woods, so the Yankees couldn't get 'em. Marster give lot of food to our soldiers, but he always kept plenty for the slaves.

Young Marster went to war and was made a captain. He was wounded but got all right to go back. He married while he was in the army, and when he went back he was wounded again. Captain Carswell took the slaves with him, but one of 'em got to cookin' for the soldiers and never did come back.

Marster always had plenty, even after the war. He freed us in May, but we didn't know what it meant. Course, some of 'em was glad, 'cause then they could go where they pleased. We all stayed with Marster 'til after Christmas, and then I worked for somebody else. I didn't get along with them, though, so I didn't stay gone but a year, and then I went back home. Marster died a few years after the war. Not long after that, the house burned, and old Miss went to live with her son, and I went off with my husband.

Charlie Hudson
*Age 80 when interviewed
in Athens, Georgia*

I WAS BORN MARCH 27, 1858, in Elbert County. Ma lived on the Bell plantation, and Marse Matt Hudson owned my pa and kept him on the Hudson place. There was seven of us chillun. Will, Bynam, John, and me was the boys, and the gals was Amanda, Liza Ann, and Gussie. 'Til us was big enough to work, us played round the house 'bout like chillun does these days.

Slave quarters was laid out like streets. Us lived in log cabins. Beds? They was just makeshift beds what was made out of pine poles. The side of the house was the head of the beds. The side rails was sharpened at both ends and driven in holes in the walls and foot posts. Then they put boards 'cross the side rails for the mattresses to lay on. The coarse-cloth bed ticks was filled with Georgia feathers. Don't you know what Georgia feathers was? Wheat straw was Georgia feathers. Our covers was sheets and plenty of good, warm quilts. Now that was at our own quarters on Marse David Bell's plantation.

Didn't everybody have as good places to sleep as us. I 'member a white family named Sims what lived in Flatwoods. They was the poorest white folks I ever seen. They had a big drove of chillun, and their pa never worked a lick in his life. He just lived on other folks' labors. Their little log cabin had a partition in it, and 'hind that partition there weren't a stitch of nothin'. They didn't have no floor but ground, and back 'hind that partition was dug out a little deeper than the rest of the house. They filled that place with leaves, and that's where all the chillun slept. Every day, Miss Sallie made 'em take out the leaves what they had slep' on the night before and fill the dugout with fresh leaves. On the other side of the partition, Miss Sallie and her old man slept 'long with their hog and hoss and cow, and that was where they cooked and ate, too. I ain't never goin' to forget them white folks.

My grandma Patsy, Pappy's ma, knocked round lookin' after the sheep and hogs close to the house, 'cause she was too old for field work. Ma's mammy was my grandma Rose. Her job was drivin' the oxcart to haul in wood from the new grounds [and] to take wheat and corn to mill and fetch back good old homemade flour and meal. I never did hear nothing 'bout my grandpas.

Ma done the cookin' for the white folks. I don't know if I was no pet, but I did stay up at the big house most of the time, and one thing I loved to do up there was to follow Miss Betsey round totin' her sewin' basket. When work got tight and hot in crop time, I helped the other chillun tote water to the hands. The bucket would slam 'gainst my leg all along the way, and most of the water would be done splashed out 'fore I got to the fields.

Marse David and his family 'most always sent their notes and messages by me and another yearlin' boy what was 'lowed to lay round the big-house yard, so us would be handy to wait on our white folks. They give you the note what they done written, and they say, "Boy, if you lose this note, you'll get a whuppin'!" All the time you was carryin' them notes, you had your whuppin' in your hand and didn't know it, unless you lost the note. I never heard of no trouble to 'mount to nothing 'tween white folks and niggers in our settlement.

Us ate good—not much different from what us does now. Most times, it was meat and bread with turnip greens, lye hominy, milk, and butter. All our cookin' was done on open fireplaces. Oh! I was fond of possums sprinkled with butter and pepper and baked down 'til the gravy was good and brown. You was lucky if you got to eat possums and gnaw the bones after my ma done cooked it.

They caught rabbits with dogs. Now and then, a crowd of niggers would jump a rabbit when no dogs was round. They would throw rocks at him and run him in a hollow log. Then they would twist him out with hickory wisps. Sometimes there weren't no fur left on the rabbit, time they got him twisted out, but that was all right. They just slapped him over dead and took him on to the cabin to be cooked. Rabbits was most generally fried.

Grown boys didn't want us chillun goin' along possum hunting with 'em, so they took off across the fields 'til they found a good, thick clump of bushes, and then they would holler out that there was some mighty fine snipes round there. They made us hold the poke [bag] open so the snipes could run in. Then they blowed out their lightwood-knot torches and left us chillun holdin' the poke, whilst they went on huntin' possums.

After dinner Saturdays, all of us took our hooks, poles, and lines down to Dry Fork Crick when it was the right time of the year to fish. Sometimes they stewed fish for old folks to eat, but young folks just loved 'em fried best.

Wintertime, they give chillun new cotton-and-wool mixed shirts what come down 'most to the ankles. By the time hot weather come, the shirt was done wore thin and shrunk up, and 'sides that, us had growed enough for 'em to be short on us, so us just wore them same shirts right on through the summer. On our place, you went barefoot 'til you was a great big yearlin'. What you wore on your head was made out of scraps of cloth they wove in the looms right there on our plantation to make pants for the grown folks.

Mr. David Bell, our marster, was born clubfooted. His hands and feet was drawed up every which way long as he lived. He was just like an old tomcat, he was such a cusser. All he done was just sit there and cuss, and a heap of time you couldn't see nothing for him to cuss about. He took his crook-handled walkin' stick and caught you and drug you up to him and then just held you tight and cussed you to your face, but he didn't ever whip nobody. Our mist'ess, Miss Betsey, was always mighty kind at times like that, and she used to give us chillun a heap of ginger cake. Their seven chillun was Dr. Bynam, Marse David, and little Misses Ad'line, Elizabeth, Mary, and Mildred. They lived in a big old two-story house, but I done forgot how it looked.

That overseer, he was a clever man, but I can't recollect his name. He never paid no heed to what sort of clothes slave wore, but he used to raise merry Cain if they didn't have good shoes to ditch [work] in. Marse David was the cussin' boss, but the overseer called hisself the whippin' boss. He had whippin's all time save up special for the women. He made 'em take off their waists, and then he whipped 'em on their bare backs 'til he was satisfied. He done all the whippin' after supper by candlelight. I don't 'member that he ever whipped a man. He just whipped women.

Everybody was up early, so that by sunrise they was out in the fields just a-whoopin' and hollerin'. At sundown, they stopped and come back to the cabins. In wheat-harvestin' time, they worked as hard as [if] they just fell out from gettin' overheated. Other times, they just worked long and steady like.

Marse David never had a carriage, so he never needed no carriage driver. He had what they called a ground sleigh. In the spring, Marse David sent a man to the woods to pick out a likely lookin' white oak saplin' and bent it down a certain way. It stayed bent that way 'til it growed big enough. Then they sawed it lengthways and put a mortise hole in each front piece to put the round through to hold the singletrees. Holes was bored at the back to fasten the plank seat to. They put a quilt on the seat for a cushion and hitched a pair of oxen to the sleigh. Come winter, come summer, snow or rain, they went right on in the old sleigh just the same!

They didn't have no jailhouse or nothin' like that round that plantation, 'cause if slaves didn't please Marster they was just made to come up to the yard at the big house and take their beatin's.

I've seen them traders come through from Virginia with two wagonloads of slaves at one time, gone down on Broad River to a place called Lisbon, where they already had orders for 'em. I ain't never seen no slaves bein' sold or auctioned off on the block.

Once, a white man named Bill Rowsey come and begged Marse David to let him teach his niggers. Marse David had the grown men swept up the cottonseed in the gin house on Sunday mornin', and for three Sundays us went to school. When us went on the fourth

Sunday, nightriders had done made a shape like a coffin in the sand out in front and painted a sign on the gin house what read, "No niggers 'lowed to be taught in this gin house." That made Marse David so mad he just cussed and cussed. He 'lowed that nobody weren't going to tell him what to do. But us was scared to go back to the gin house to school. Next week, Marse David had 'em build a brush arbor down by the creek, but when us went down there on Sunday for school us found the nightriders had done destroyed the brush arbor, and that was the end of my going to school.

There weren't no church for slaves where us was. Marse David give us a pass so us wouldn't be disturbed and let us go round from one plantation to another on Sundays for prayer meetin's in the cabins and under trees, if the weather was warm and nice. Sometimes when there was a jubilee comin' off, slaves was 'lowed to go to their marster's church. The chillun had to take a backseat while the old folks done all the singin', so I never learned none of them songs good 'nough to 'member what the words was, or the tunes neither. Now and then, us went to a funeral—not often. But if there was a baptizin' inside of ten miles round from where us lived, us didn't miss it. Us knowed how to walk and went to get the pleasure.

After slaves got in from the fields at night, the women cooked supper while the men chopped wood. Unless the crops was in the grass mighty bad or somethin' else was awful urgent, there wasn't no work done after dinner on Saturdays. The old folks ironed, cleaned house, and the like, and the young folks went out Saturday night and danced to the music what they made beatin' on tin pans. Sundays, youngsters went to the woods and hunted hicker [hickory] nuts and muscadine. The old folks stayed home and looked one another's heads over for nits and lice. Whenever they found anything, they mashed it between their finger and thumb and went ahead searchin'. Then the womans wrapped each other's hair the way it was to stay fixed 'til the next Sunday.

Christmas, us went from house to house lookin' for locust and persimmon beer. Chillun went to all the houses huntin' gingerbread. Ma used to roll it thin, cut it out with a thimble, and give a dozen of them little balls to each chile. Persimmon beer and gingerbread! What big times us did have at Christmas.

New Year's Day, they raked up the horse and cow lots if the weather was good. Marster just made us work enough on New Year's Day to call it workin', so he could say he made us start the New Year right.

Marse David had corn shuckin's what lasted two or three weeks at a time. They had a general to keep them brash boys straight. The number of generals depended on how much corn us had and how many slaves was shuckin' corn. After it was all shucked, there was a big celebration in store for the slaves. They cooked up wash pots full of lamb, pork, and beef and had collard greens that was worth lookin' at. They had water buckets full of whiskey. When them niggers danced after all that eatin' and drinkin', it wasn't rightly dancin'; it was wrestlin'.

Them moonlight cotton pickin's was big old times. They give prizes to the ones pickin' the most cotton. The prizes was apt to be a quart of whiskey for the man what picked the most and a dress for the woman what was ahead. Them niggers wouldn't take no time to empty cotton in baskets—just dropped it out quick on baggin' in the field.

They went from one plantation to another to quiltin's. After the women got through quiltin' and ate a big dinner, then they asked the men to come in and dance with 'em.

Whenever any of our white folks' gals got married, there was two or three weeks of celebratin'. What a time us did have if it was one of our own little misses gettin' married! When they arrived, it was something else. The white folks was dressed up to beat the band, and all the slaves was up on their toes to do everything just right and to see all they could. After the preacher done finished his words to the young couple, then they had the wedding feast! There was all sorts of meat to choose from at weddin' dinners—turkeys, geese, chickens, peafowls, and guineas, not to mention good old hams and other meats.

Pitchin' hoss shoes and playin' marbles was heaps and lots of fun when I was growin' up. After while, the old folks decided them games was gamblin' and wouldn't let us play no more.

I don't know nothin' 'bout no ghosties. Us had enough to be scared of without takin' up no time with that sort of thing.

When Marse David changed me from calf shepherd to cowboy, he sent three or four of us boys to drive the cows to a good place to graze, 'cause the male beast was so mean and bad 'bout gettin' after chillun, he thought if he sent enough of us there wouldn't be no trouble. Them days, there wasn't no fence law, and calves was just turned loose on the pasture to graze. The first time I went by myself to drive the cows off to graze and come back with them, Aunt Vinnie reported a bunch of the cows was missin'—'bout twenty of 'em when she done the milkin' that night. And I had to go back huntin' them cows. The moon come out bright and clear, but I couldn't see them cows nowhere—didn't even hear the bell cow. After while, I was standin' in the mayberry field a-lookin' across Dry Fork Crick, and there was them cows. The bell was pulled so close on the bell cow's neck where she was caught in the bushes that it couldn't ring. I looked at them cows, then I looked at the crick, where I could see snakes as thick as the fingers on your hand. But I knew I had to get them cows back home, so I just lit out and loped 'cross that crick so fast them snakes never had no chance to bite me. That was the worst racket I ever got in.

Marse David and Miss Betsey took mighty good care of their niggers, 'specially when they was sick. Dr. Bynam Bell, their oldest son, was a doctor, but Miss Betsey was a powerful good hand at doctoring herself. She looked after all the slave women. For medicines, they give us asafiddy [asafetida], calomel, and castor oil more than anything else for our different ailments.

Marse David's nephew, Mr. Henry Bell, visited at the big house durin' the war, and he was cut down just a few days after he left us and went back to the battlefield.

Us had been hearing first one thing and another 'bout Freedom might come, when one mornin' Mr. Will Bell, a patteroller, come ridin' out on his hoss at top speed through the rye field where us was at work. Us made sure he was after some poor slave, 'til he yelled out, "What you niggers workin' for? Don't you know you is free as jaybirds?" 'Bout that time, the trumpet blowed for dinner, and us fell in line a-marchin' to the big house. Marse David said, "You-all might just as well be free as anybody else." Then he promised to give us somethin' to eat and wear if us would stay on with him, and there us did stay for 'bout three years after the war.

Where us lived, Ku Kluxers was called "night thiefs." They stole money and weapons from niggers after the war. They took fifty dollars in gold from me and fifty dollars in Jeff Davis shinplasters from my brother. Pa and Ma had left that money for us to use when us got big enough. A few niggers managed somehow to buy a little land.

It was a God-sent method Mr. Lincoln used to give us our Freedom. Mr. Davis didn't want no war, and he opposed it all he knowed how, but if he hadn't gone ahead and fought there never would have been nothin' done for us.

In a way, I'm satisfied with what confronts me. A person in jail or on the chain gang would rather be outside and free than in captivity. That's how I feel.

I done been here a long time. I done seen many come and go. Lots of changes has took place. All that recollectin' sure took me back over many a rocky road, but them was the days ain't never going to be no more.